PLAY BETTER
HOCKEY

PLAY BETTER
HOCKEY

Ron Davidson
Foreword by Ron MacLean

FIREFLY BOOKS

A FIREFLY BOOK

Published by Firefly Books Ltd. 2010

First Printing

Publisher Cataloging-in-Publication Data (U.S.)
Davidson, Ron.
    Play better hockey : 50 essential skills for player development /
Ron Davidson.
[ ] p. : ill., col. photos. ; cm.
Summary: A collection of more than 50 skills to help players of all levels
improve their game. Covers skating, stick work and dekeing.
ISBN-13: 978-1-55407-638-3 (pbk.)   ISBN-10: 1-55407-638-2 (pbk.)
ISBN-13: 978-1-55407-568-3 (bound)   ISBN-10: 1-55407-568-8 (bound)
1. Hockey—Training. I. Title.
796.96207 dc22   GV848.3.D38 2010

Library and Archives Canada Cataloguing in Publication
Davidson, Ron, 1957–
    Play better hockey : 50 essential skills for player development /
Ron Davidson.
ISBN-13: 978-1-55407-638-3 (pbk.)   ISBN-10: 1-55407-638-2 (pbk.)
ISBN-13: 978-1-55407-568-3 (bound)   ISBN-10: 1-55407-568-8 (bound)
    1. Hockey—Training. I. Title.
GV848.3.D38 2010   796.962'2   C2010-901196-1

Published in the United States by
Firefly Books (U.S.) Inc.
P.O. Box 1338, Ellicott Station
Buffalo, New York 14205

Cover and interior design by
Gareth Lind, LINDdesign

Printed in Canada

Published in Canada by
Firefly Books Ltd.
66 Leek Crescent
Richmond Hill, Ontario L4B 1H1

*The publisher gratefully acknowledges the financial support for our publishing
program by the Canada Book Fund as administered by the Department of
Canadian Heritage.*

Erik Johnson executes a heel turn.
See page 120 for more on attacking
with a heel turn.

Contents

John Tavares executes the backhand variation of the Vincent Lecavalier Special. See page 126 to find out more.

Foreword

⊙ **Ron MacLean**

A few years ago I was asking NHL star Mike Foligno if there was a common thread among players who possess a great shot. Mike said that the first tip-off for him was if the player had thick wrists.

You might be thinking, "Great, I don't have thick wrists," but Mike went on to explain that whether you are born with thick wrists or not isn't as important as developing strength in your forearms and wrists through good old-fashioned practice. His secret drill? Mike would line up 100 pucks in a semicircle across the top of the slot. He'd then shoot all 100 in succession without taking a break. Mike said he would bury his head and not even look at the net, continuing to fire away until he was finished. Very few people, he commented, would make it through the 100 pucks successively without stopping for a break.

I told Don Cherry and Harry Neale this story while the three of us sat in the stands at the Saddledome with a group of young players from the WHL's Calgary Hitmen. We were watching the Calgary Flames at their morning skate when I repeated Foligno's take on thick wrists, followed by his shooting 100 pucks. I added that I thought it was interesting that Mike didn't bother to look at the net and instead just buried his head when he shot. Grapes quipped, "No kidding? Big deal. The net hasn't moved in a hundred years!" Everyone laughed. And while Don is right, I think it is important to remember that Mike was building more than just thick wrists with his 100-puck routine. Mike undoubtedly developed a strong shot, but he also would have created an innate feel for the net and where it was in relation to his position on the ice. He also more than likely developed a quickness that aided him in so many of his 727 NHL points. Thick wrists are wonderful, but with every exercise there are hidden benefits and surprise results, something to keep in mind when practicing the skills in this book.

A few years later *Hockey Night in Canada* brought together a group of 15 coaches, players and teachers to brainstorm for a new feature we were developing called "Think Hockey."

The feature was to be a hockey tips segment that blended individual skill and team play, which would be taught to viewers by professionals. It would air twice nightly on HNIC. Among our guest experts was Ron Davidson, who had turned heads with his revolutionary teaching methods in a program he called UltraSkills. Ron was very passionate about the core fundamentals of skating and body positioning, which he attests, when taught properly to players, can allow players of any level to execute high-skill maneuvers.

In the meetings Ron got on a roll discussing how players can effectively use their inside and outside edges while skating. I remember Ron explaining how Wayne Gretzky actually accelerated through his tight turns by placing pressure on the outside edge of the foot that was leading the turn and on the inside edge of the foot that was trailing the turn. After what was, to me, a spellbinding five-minute description of Gretzky's outside-edge, inside-edge turn, Brian Kilrea, the Hall of Fame coach of the Ottawa 67's deadpanned, "You mean he glides!" We all laughed. But no one more than Ron because it was literally that simple, yet it remains today something that not many players or coaches completely understand. I knew at that instant I was going to really enjoy working with Ron on "Think Hockey." He is incredibly good-natured and he knows his stuff. We had a lot of laughs shooting the tips for HNIC. I can't tell you how many times Ron's expertise has helped NHL coaches and players come to a fuller understanding of the tips or skills they were teaching. As a result of working with Ron my own skating improved. The figure skaters on *Battle of the Blades* often remarked about my edge work, and I got it all from Ron. (Especially the cross-unders on page 43!)

From Mike Foligno to me to you, I encourage you to just bury your head … in these pages. You are about to give hockey your best shot, and, in my opinion, if you want to play better hockey, Ron Davidson is certainly the teacher for you.

Introduction

I have loved this incredible game for as long as I can remember. With our skates already on, my brother and I would walk on the snow-covered road a few short blocks to the corner rink in Graham Park in Nepean, near Ottawa, Ontario, and spend hours playing. My dad tells me that there were many nights that he would come down to the rink, long after I was supposed to be home, and find me still wheeling around the ice. Sometimes I'd be by myself, sometimes with my brother, but I was always oblivious to the time. "You've got to come home," he would say, "before you freeze your toes off!"

In the winter of 1974, a few months before I was selected in the first round of the Quebec Major Junior Hockey League draft by the Cornwall Royals, my assistant coach in Midget, Tom Meeker, asked me what I was doing that summer and said, "My brother Howie runs a pretty good hockey school and he's looking for staff." During that first summer I discovered that I loved to teach hockey. Tom's invitation led to 12 summers of me working with one of the true masters of skill development—Howie Meeker was a great mentor. In my pursuit of an understanding of hockey technique, I couldn't have asked for a better beginning.

During those same years, I benefited from the instruction of some of Canada's best technical coaches: Brian Kilrea when I played for the Ottawa 67's in 1976–77, and Tom Watt, Clare Drake, George Kingston and Dave King when I played for Canada's National Team from 1978–83 (which included the Olympics in Lake Placid in 1980). When I played pro hockey for Vastra Frolunda in the Swedish Elite League, I was exposed to Swedish training programs. When I played pro in Switzerland, I had a Czechoslovakian coach.

I became a student of the game. I craved to learn as much as I could about how players developed hockey skills. Why do some players develop great glide while others don't? What is the secret to extreme speed on skates? Why does the puck seem to explode off of some player's sticks when they shoot and not others? I found that if I wanted the answers to these questions I needed to watch elite players and understand what they did to perform on the ice.

As a member of Canada's national program, I had the opportunity to play against some of the best players in the world. In 1978, when Father David Bauer was rekindling the program, which had been dormant for a decade, we played the Edmonton Oilers of the WHA, with their young

star Wayne Gretzky. After playing against him, I realized that Wayne was totally unappreciated as a skater. His puck skills were incredible, but what really amazed me was his ability to move laterally, to accelerate through tight glide turns like no one else and to execute seamless transitions while always facing the play. Wayne was a true artist on skates and the ice was his canvas. He was able to move his feet and contact the ice to accomplish exactly what he wanted.

In 1979 I was selected for the 1980 Canadian Olympic Team. We flew to Prague, Czechoslovakia, in September of 1979 to play in the Rude Pravo tournament, a feature tournament for the top national hockey teams. The Soviet national team was a formidable team comprised of some of the very best Soviet players in their prime, including Vladislav Tretiak, Viacheslav Fetisov and one of the most explosive players I had ever seen—Valeri Kharlamov. I remember the first time I saw the Soviets practice. Bobby Orr was traveling with our team as an ambassador. He walked out to ice level with us to watch the Soviets practice. When we returned to our dressing room, the silence was deafening. None of us had ever seen a team practice at that level of speed or intensity. Bobby read the room immediately. "You've got to be kidding me, you're not worried about those guys are you?" he said, pointing toward the ice. "It's all done with smoke and mirrors. Sure they look good in practice, but they are totally different in the games."

"What do you mean?" piped Glenn Anderson, my right winger. Bobby's quick answer was, "I mean they're a hell of a lot faster!"

On the heels of the 1972 Summit Series, the North American hockey community was beginning to realize that there was still a lot left to learn about the game. Before that famous series, the scouting report on the Soviets was that "they didn't even know which foot to shoot off," commenting on their tendency to shoot off their same foot. What no one realized then was how effective a shooting technique this was, allowing a player to shoot in motion and to release the puck with deception. In fact, what was forgotten was that two of the NHL's most dangerous scorers, Rocket Richard and Gordie Howe, had used the exact same technique. Now every elite player knows that he or she needs to have this ability in order to be successful.

The game continues to evolve, and it is the courage to question old ways of thought and the desire to be progressive in our approach to skill development that will allow the game to grow. The American "Miracle on Ice" in 1980 did not happen because the players were "feeding the wolf," as suggested in the Disney movie. The Canadian national team played the Americans many times leading up to the Olympics. Early on, we beat them in convincing fashion. As the Olympics approached, the gap between us seemed to be closing fast. I was fascinated by some of the innovative training techniques that they used, on and off the ice, which were designed to inspire a creative offensive approach. In preparing for the Soviets, instead of trying to neutralize a superior opponent, Herb Brooks was intent on the American players raising their game collectively to a point where they could compete with one of the greatest teams ever assembled. It was a long shot, but when all the stars were aligned, it worked. The game has come a long way since that miracle on ice, but as players and as coaches, our approach should continue to be innovative, to challenge ourselves and to raise our skills. Ultimately, we should be striving to play a better brand of hockey.

The greatest players in the game have always done this—and we need to follow their lead. I ran a clinic in Ottawa the day before the 2005 NHL draft to showcase the skills of the five players who were expected to be the top five picks in the draft, Sidney Crosby included. I designed a few drills to showcase his incredible acceleration and superb skating technique. What amazed me about Sidney was that even in a clinic that was essentially a media event, he was totally focused on getting the most out of the drills. He wanted to try new things, to push the envelope, to go even faster. The year before, Hayley Wickenheiser, one of the greatest female players in the world, was a guest instructor at one of my hockey schools for elite girls. Before long, she was jumping into the drills and trying the skating exercises. "I like the emphasis on quick transition and being light on your skates" she told me. "I could use that in my game!" It was obvious why she had reached the pinnacle of women's hockey. She never stopped learning.

Many elite athletes do not understand what they do technically that separates them from other players. Their hockey skills have become second nature. In 1981, Howie Meeker asked me to work with NHL players in order to instruct them on how to teach hockey to kids for the segment "Pro-Tips" for *Hockey Night in Canada*, and it was a real eye opener for me … and for them! I outlined the skill progressions to Mark Messier, Denis Savard, Bobby Smith, Larry Robinson, Mike Bossy and others. The players were to then illustrate the skills on TV. Each player, without exception, indicated how helpful it was to break the skills down and that they would have benefited from the knowledge at an earlier age. They also said they would try to work it into their practices in the future. Thirty years later, from 2006–09, I was involved in coordinating the material for the skill segments show "Think Hockey" with Ron MacLean, which also aired on *Hockey Night in Canada*. I was the on-ice hockey director, and I worked with some of the NHL's top coaches and players —people like Mike Babcock, Dave Tippett, Lindy Ruff, Randy Carlyle, Paul Maurice, Wendel Clark, Adrian Aucoin and Larry Murphy—to present segments on individual and team skills and concepts important to the game. And while the game has certainly changed in three decades, the message remains the same: every player, regardless of age or ability, can improve their skills and can play better hockey.

It doesn't matter whether I am teaching beginners or pros, young players or old timers, girls or boys. The principles of technique and the skill progressions are the same. The difference in specific instruction depends on where the individual player is on the continuum of hockey development. As you strive to learn, your focus must be on the game itself: an incredible sport that demands an athlete to learn two extensions of the body—skates on the ice and a puck on the end of a stick. It is a combination of skating and puck skills, which, when coupled with vision and a sense for the game, culminates in the incredible athletic achievement we witness as hockey. And if acquiring a physical skill can be satisfying, then the network of skills that can be learned in hockey can offer untold enrichment. No matter your skill level, the better you get, the more you will enjoy everything hockey has to offer.

I sincerely hope this book helps you to connect to this beautiful game. There is no doubt that after reading this book and watching professional players use the techniques outlined within, you will come to a better understanding of how your body has to move to perform specific hockey skills. You will then be well on your way to achieving our goal for you —namely, to play better hockey!

1 Gearing Up

Daniel Alfredsson tapes his stick before a game. See page 23 for more on how to tape your stick.

Skate Blades

What Is a Skate Blade?

A skate blade is thin and two-edged, made of stainless steel and mounted in a holder that is fastened with rivets to a skate boot. Each blade is contoured from toe to heel, which means that not all of your blade is on the ice at the same time. Each blade also has a concave groove running between the two edges, known as a hollow, which gives a skate an inside and an outside edge.

Edges and Hollows

Edges provide control, and without them you would slip and slide. Having two edges with a hollow in between allows you to carve, draw or push off the ice with either the inside or outside of your blade, and it also allows you to glide. Glide is the direct result of the hollow's low level of friction as compared to the edges, which have a relatively high level of friction.

When you are coasting on the ice you are running on the edges of your blades and—depending on your weight, the pressure you apply and the ice conditions—the hollow of your blade. The deeper the hollow, the deeper the edges, and the more you will be running on your edges and the less you will be running on the hollow. This means more friction, which gives you more grip but less glide. The shallower the hollow, the more you are running on your hollow, which means less friction and more glide. Some friction is good, as it produces heat, which contributes

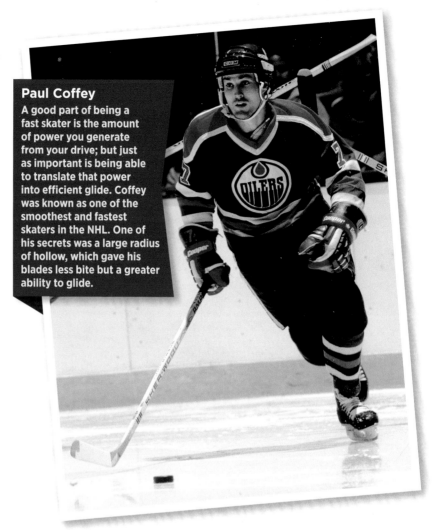

Paul Coffey
A good part of being a fast skater is the amount of power you generate from your drive; but just as important is being able to translate that power into efficient glide. Coffey was known as one of the smoothest and fastest skaters in the NHL. One of his secrets was a large radius of hollow, which gave his blades less bite but a greater ability to glide.

to glide. Too much friction, however, hampers glide.

Radius of Hollow

Radius of hollow (ROH) is the technical term to describe the depth of the hollow between a blade's edges. This measurement reflects the length of the radius of a circle, a portion of which forms the hollow between the edges: a small radius indicates a small circle and a deep hollow, while a large radius indicates a large circle and a shallow hollow. And so, a blade with a small ROH has a deep hollow that gives you less glide, but you will

have more bite from your edges, enabling you to turn sharper and start more quickly. A blade with a large ROH gives you a shallower hollow, so the blade is closer to being flat between the edges, allowing you to glide better.

The radius of hollow typically used by NHLers is becoming larger as players recognize and appreciate the value of glide. Only a short time ago, most NHL players used an ROH of $1/2$ inch. More recently, the trend has been for NHL players to use a higher ROH, moving toward $5/8$ inch and even $3/4$ inch. Paul Coffey, one of the greatest skaters to play the game and an excellent glider, used an ROH of at least 1 inch and typically much higher. In fact, the entire Edmonton Oiler team that won Stanley Cups in the 1980s used, on average, higher ROHs than other teams to promote glide and skating performance. Because of the larger ice surface they play on, European players are accustomed to very high ROHs of up to $1^1/_2$ inches, and many continue to use them in the NHL. Bandy (a hockey-like sport that is played on a very large ice surface) has players who use very high ROHs in order to maximize glide. Some NHL players will ask the team trainer to adjust the ROH of their blades slightly depending on the nature of the ice in a particular rink. Sidney Crosby, for example, typically uses an ROH of $^7/_{16}$ inch but will experiment with a higher ROH depending on the circumstances.

An ideal ROH will allow you to strike a balance between glide and maneuverability. The key to finding your preferred ROH is to start at a relatively moderate ROH, such as $^1/_2$ inch, and try increasing the ROH in increments of $^1/_{16}$ inch. If you find that you want more bite and less glide, experiment by decreasing the ROH. When choosing an ROH, remember to take into account your ability, your playing style and your size, along with the ice conditions you are expecting—the ice NHLers play on is typically softer than your local rink or outdoor surface, and soft

ice is friendlier to skate blades. The softer the ice, the more bite you will have, so it allows you to experiment with a higher ROH to improve your glide. Your weight is also an important factor. Heavier players will still have bite with higher ROHs. Lighter players may need lower ROHs because they need to increase the impact of their edges.

In terms of keeping your skate blade's edge, a deeper hollow exposes your edges more than a shallow hollow does, leading to a higher likelihood of nicks or burrs. Your skates will also become dull more quickly with a deep hollow. The shallower the ROH of the blade, the less likely it is to be compromised and the longer it will keep it's edge. This means that,

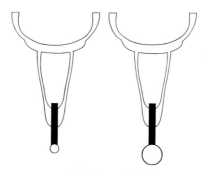

FIG. 1 & 2 Radius of Hollow
In these skate cutaways (in which you can see the boot, blade holder and blade—which is black), the ROH is represented by the circle at the bottom of the blade. The smaller circle represents a small ROH, while the larger circle represents a large ROH. The smaller the ROH, the deeper the hollow and the more edge you will have. The larger the ROH, the shallower the hollow and the more glide you will be able to generate.

typically, players with a deeper hollow (a low ROH) should get their skates sharpened more often than players with a shallow hollow (a high ROH). Some NHL players with low ROHs get their skates sharpened between periods or after every game. Players with high ROHs might only get their skates sharpened after many games.

It should be noted that most players get their skates sharpened too often. You want to get your skates sharpened often enough for them to have consistent edges with consistent glide and bite. If your blades are protected off the ice and don't receive any nicks during the ice session—from contact with the goal post, other skates or composite sticks—they should remain consistently sharp for long periods of ice use, especially if you use a higher ROH. When checking your blades, make sure your edges are even. To check this, flip your skate over and place a dime on the blade so that it sits across both edges—if the skate is held straight the dime should be level. Even edges will allow you to glide on a side-to-side flat blade, meaning you will have equal pressure on both edges.

Blade Radius

Player skates (as opposed to goalie skates) are often referred to as being "rockered," which means the blade is contoured, or not flat. The manufacturer does not preset contouring, and every new pair of skates has to be contoured before use. The technical term referring to the contour of the blade is blade radius, and this operates on the same principal as radius of hollow: the measure of the radius is the measure of the circumference of a circle with a portion of that circle being the blade. Unlike radius of hollow, which is measured in inches, blade radius is measured in feet. The larger the radius, the less contoured the blade is and the more blade you will have in contact with the ice; the smaller the radius, the more contoured the blade is and the less blade you will have in contact with the ice. The more blade you have on the ice, the more impact your blade will have on your speed. Speed skaters, for example, use the longest blades possible while still allowing for quick starts and cross-over turns. The typical blade radius for a hockey player is 9 feet, but it can range from 6 to 13 feet. For goalies it is much higher since the blade is much flatter. Wayne

Blade Radius: Speed Skates
Speed skates have a very large blade radius that allows as much blade as possible to be on the ice. With so much blade on the ice, speed skaters experience increased glide, which in turn increases speed.

Gretzky, who put a high premium on maneuverability, used a small blade radius of 7 feet, which gave the Great One less blade on the ice. He sacrificed some straightaway speed in order to maximize agility.

NHL players have been steadily moving toward blades with a larger radius in order to get more blade in contact with the ice so they can achieve greater speeds. When deciding the radius for your skates, you should aim to have as large a radius as possible without sacrificing your maneuverability. As you gain experience, you can experiment with your blade radius and push toward a larger radius. Improving your skating technique, including your hand and body position, will allow you to be agile while using a larger blade radius. More importantly, using a large blade radius will offer you more glide (and more speed) in and out of turns and transitions. The radius for younger, smaller skaters will be shorter than for larger adult skaters simply because of the differences in the overall length of their blades. In any case, it is extremely

important that the contour of your blade is centered. This will give you maximum balance, and it will allow you to apply equal force through the heels and balls of your feet when you thrust.

The Relationship Between Radius of Hollow and Blade Radius

The relationship between blade radius and radius of hollow is where you can do your fine-tuning. For example, some players will use a large blade radius (for greater speed) combined with a small radius of hollow (for more bite for turning and starts), while other players will use a small blade radius (for better maneuverability) with a large radius of hollow (for better glide). Take your skill, technique, style of play and physical size into account when you choose the

FIG. 3 Blade Radius
An example of a large blade radius. The flatter the contour (large blade radius), the more blade you have on the ice to contribute to glide, which will contribute to speed. With a smaller blade radius (rounder contour), you will have enhanced agility but will sacrifice some ability to glide.

characteristics for your blades. Heavier players can take advantage of the increased glide of a large blade radius and may also find performance benefits from a large ROH, as their weight will give their blades more bite, even with smaller edges. Lighter players can use a smaller ROH to get bite for turning and starting but may want a large blade radius to maximize their straightaway speed.

Pitch of the Skate

The pitch of the skate is the angle of the foot relative to the blade on the ice, and it is determined by the position of the blade holder, which is attached to the bottom of the skate. Some blade holders are positioned so that your foot sits flat, while others are positioned so that your feet and the rest of your body naturally lean forward. Different makes of skates will have different pitches. The pitch can be changed by changing the blade holder or by inserting "lifts" to a portion of the skate's insole. Pitch is a matter of personal preference and does not depend on whether you play defense or forward.

When choosing the pitch of your skates, remember that the proper hockey-skating position is on a flat blade with a forward body lean, whether you are skating forward or backward. It is also important to note that while you will thrust from both the balls and heels of your feet, it is quite often the balls of your feet that do the most thrusting. For instance, you thrust from the

balls of your feet when executing a forward stride, backward stride, cross-overs and cross-unders, and the majority of the moves you'll do while agility skating involve thrusting from the balls of your feet. Therefore, a forward pitch is highly recommended. If you are skating with a forward pitch, be mindful not to glide only on the balls of your feet—maintain a good body position so that you skate on a flat blade with your weight evenly distributed between your heels and the balls of your feet.

FIG. 4 Blade Pitch
This skate is pitched forward, with the heel higher than the ball of the foot. Many skates are pitched forward, as the natural skating position is to be on a flat blade with a forward body lean.

Debunking the Myths

At one time it was believed that the position you played should influence the characteristics of the blade you used. For example, defensemen were advised to use a large blade radius for stability and straightaway speed, both backward and forward, while forwards were told to use a smaller blade radius for better maneuverability and agility. Defensemen often used a skate pitch that put them sitting back on their heels, to help them skate backward, while the pitch for forwards' skates was toward the balls of their feet, to help them move forward more quickly. The ROH recommended for forwards was deep for more bite during quick turns, while defensemen were advised to use a shallow hollow for more glide and speed while going straight, forward or backward.

As technical instruction has progressed, it is now understood that the position you play should not dictate the blade you use. All players, regardless of their position, need to be as quick, agile and maneuverable as possible and maintain maximum glide for speed. Honing your technical skating skills and body position is important because it allows you to take advantage of the characteristics of your blades and benefit from maximum glide without sacrificing maneuverability. Further, the advantages of glide are being recognized more and more. "Power skating" is a misnomer, since glide is as important as power when it comes to skating performance. In particular, glide into and out of transitions and turns can dramatically affect your overall agility and your ability to execute skating maneuvers.

Stick Selection

Stick Flex
Andrei Markov releases a slap shot with the aid of the flexion of his composite stick. Stick flex creates whip when shooting, and whip creates speed.

The Case for Wood

Most players in the NHL use one-piece composite sticks. Very few players use wooden sticks, but those that prefer wood, like Jason Spezza, are often very good puckhandlers. The majority of the players currently playing in the NHL grew up using wooden sticks or two-piece sticks with a wooden blade and/or plug.

All players can improve their puckhandling skills by using a wooden stick or blade, which will improve their feel for the puck. "Feel" is a player's sense of where the puck is on the stick and how the stick is moving the puck; feel is transferred through the stick to the player's hands. This sense, or message, from the puck to the player is clearest when transferred

through wood to sensitive parts of the hand, such as the palm and the tip of the little finger. Like a fisher who is trying to sense what a lure is doing at the end of a fishing line, hockey players will have a better sense of what the puck is doing on the blade of their stick when using the proper grip and a wooden stick. For these reasons, using a wooden stick or attaching a wooden blade and/or a wooden plug or extension to a composite shaft will improve your feel for the puck. This will allow you to learn puck skills more quickly and to grasp more advanced puck skills more easily.

The Case for Composite

Using a composite stick can improve your ability to shoot. First off, a composite stick is often lighter than a wooden stick, allowing you to move your hands more quickly, which can translate into a quicker release and a faster shot. Secondly, a composite stick typically has more flex than a wooden stick, and the more your stick flexes the more whip it will have, which contributes to the speed of your shot. Thirdly, the materials in the blade and shaft of a composite stick are designed to produce more "kick," or power from the blade and shaft into the shot. Finally, the one-piece design of a composite stick allows a more direct transfer of power from the player through the stick to the puck.

Having reviewed how a composite stick can contribute to the speed of your shot, it is important to note that some of the players who have recorded the fastest shots in the NHL did so using wooden sticks, including Al MacInnis and Adrian Aucoin, who both won the hardest-shot competition during the All-Star Game weekend with wooden sticks.

Stick Size

The shaft and blade of your stick should be the right size for you. One of the most common mistakes made by younger players and beginners is to use a stick that is too big, too stiff in the shaft and too long and thick in the blade. Sticks range in size from youth to junior to intermediate to senior, and each has a progressively larger blade and bigger shaft (both circumference and length). If you're learning to puckhandle, or wish to improve your puckhandling, it is crucial that you select a stick you can handle easily and that maximizes your feel for the puck. Young players should not use a senior stick. Beginners should use a stick with a blade that is straight or has a slight and gradual curve and that is as thin and flexible as possible. The thinner and more flexible the blade, the more feel of the puck it will transfer to its user. The shaft of your stick should be thin enough so that you can handle and move it quickly. If a stick with the proper size of shaft is not long enough for you, add a wooden plug to the shaft to extend the stick's length.

Ideally all players, and particularly beginners, should use a stick that is no longer than half an inch below their chin when they are on skates and the stick is positioned upright with the toe of the blade touching the ice. Many elite players have sticks that are considerably shorter than this. As you become more experienced, you can learn to handle the puck with a longer

FIG. 5 Stick Lie
The further your stick is from your body when gripped properly with your blade flat on the ice, the greater the angle of the blade will be in relation to the shaft. A hockey stick with a large lie angle (a) is referred to as a low lie, while a small lie (b) is a high lie.

stick, which has the advantage of more reach. Martin St. Louis is an example of a skilled NHL puckhandler who uses a longer stick. However, most players still prefer to use a shorter stick. A shorter stick enables you to handle the puck in the proper position, with your hands toward the center and in front of your body. Having a shorter stick also allows you to move your top hand across your body with ease, enabling you to keep the blade square to the ice as you puckhandle on either side of your body when you are in tight turns and when the puck is at your feet.

Stick Lie

The last aspect in determining the right stick for you is the lie of a stick: the angle of the blade in relation to the shaft. A blade with a proper lie is square to the ice when you are in the hockey-playing position (see page 26). Players who carry the puck closer to their body will use a higher lie (six), while players who handle the puck away from their body will use a lower lie (four).

Stick Grip

Top-Hand Grip

There is only one proper way to hold your hockey stick with your top hand, and improper top-hand grip may be the single most common problem among players learning the game. Proper top-hand grip is crucial to control the stick while skating and, ultimately, to control and handle the puck. Using the proper top-hand grip will also help you position your stick properly and, through that, help you to achieve proper body placement. The ability to control your stick and to move it quickly into the proper position is crucial to mastering skating maneuvers.

It is best to learn the top-hand grip without gloves on first, in order to see and feel where the top of the stick is in your hand. To place your top hand properly, hold it out as if to shake someone's hand. Next place the very top of the stick in your palm, with the butt end against the heel of your hand, directly below your third finger. Then wrap your hand around the stick so there is no space between your little finger and the top of the stick. Grip your little finger and third finger tightly together and around the stick; the pressure applied by these two fingers will allow you to control your stick. Wrap your middle and index fingers, along with your thumb, loosely around the stick. When wrapped around the stick, the area between your index finger and thumb should create a V-shape, with the point of the "V" resting in

FIG. 6 Proper Top-Hand Grip (Side)

When seen from the side, the butt end of the shaft should sit against the heel of your palm and your last two fingers wrapped tightly around the knob of the shaft. Your wrist should be relaxed and pointing slightly downward.

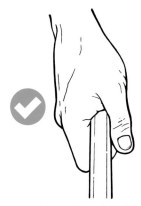

FIG. 7 Proper Top-Hand Grip (Front)

When seen from the front, your thumb and forefinger should create a "V" that rests in the middle of the front of the shaft.

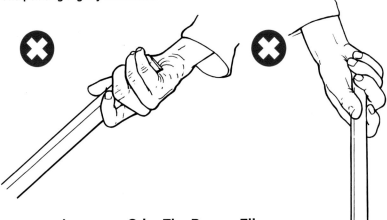

FIG. 8 & 9 Improper Grip: The Burger Flipper

This is NOT how to hold a hockey stick. This is how you hold a spatula! This grip will make it impossible for you to hold your stick straight with your blade square to the ice, and it will make it very difficult to roll your wrists — the key movement in puckhandling, passing and shooting.

the middle of the front of the shaft when the stick is at your side and the heel of the blade is on the ice.

A common mistake among beginners is to roll their top hand around the stick so that the "V" is resting on the side of the shaft and not the front—a grip we call the "burger flipper." This grip will hamper your ability to handle the puck, to shoot the puck and even to hold your stick straight. Remember, the stick is not a spatula!

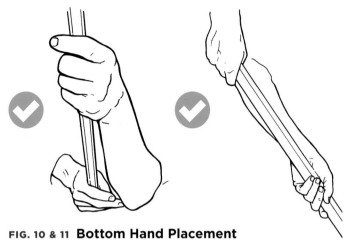

FIG. 10 & 11 Bottom Hand Placement
Your bottom hand is in the proper position (for the hockey-playing position)
if the elbow of your bottom hand is up against your top hand when your forearm
is placed along the shaft of your stick.

Bottom-Hand Grip

Bottom hand placement and grip should change as play dictates. When you are handling the puck, your bottom hand should generally remain loose and flexible so you can easily move it up and down the shaft. Your bottom hand must grip more tightly if you are handling the puck with only your bottom hand on the stick or when extra firmness will help you protect the puck from stick checks. When passing, your grip with your bottom hand should be firm. Your grip should be tight when shooting.

You will often change the position of your bottom hand on the stick, but there is an ideal bottom-hand position for puckhandling when the puck is in front of you and in the middle of your body. Here is a little trick to use to make sure your bottom hand is in the right position when you are in the hockey-playing position:

1 Using the proper top-hand grip, lock your top hand on the top of the stick.
2 Place your bottom hand just beneath your top hand, on the stick.
3 Slide your bottom hand down the shaft—keeping your forearm and elbow close to the shaft as you move your hand—until the elbow of your bottom arm meets your top hand. Lock your bottom hand at this point.
4 Move into the hockey-playing position, with your top hand close to the middle of and in front of your body.

Taping the Shaft of Your Stick

A small knob created with a few turns of tape is best. Avoid excessive "grip" tape at the top of the stick, as there shouldn't be any space between your little finger and the top of your stick. You also need to "feel" the puck through the knob and the stick, and the less tape there is the better your feel for the puck will be. Less tape also makes it easier for you to rotate the stick with your top hand, which is crucial for puckhandling. As well, avoid any tape on the shaft so you can freely slide your bottom hand up and down it.

Taping the Blade of Your Stick

Tape from heel to toe. A strip of tape along the bottom of a wooden stick will help protect the blade from wear. Some players love white tape, but black has advantages: it makes it more difficult for players, including goalies, to see where the puck is on your stick, and the goalie may (even briefly) lose a puck in flight against a background of black tape.

2 Skating Essentials

**Scott Niedermayer executes a perfect
forward stride. See page 28 for the
principles of great skating.**

Balance and Positioning

Developing great balance on skates is perhaps, athletically, the single most important building block to becoming an elite player. You need balance to perform all of the tasks necessary to play hockey: it allows you to execute the proper skating techniques and maximize glide and power, and it gives you the stability and foundation required to puckhandle, pass and shoot. Most importantly, balance allows you to integrate skating with stick-work and perform movements that will allow you to accomplish what you want, when you want, on the ice.

You achieve balance through proper body position and a "flat blade." In the hockey-playing position and the hockey-skating position, your skate blade should be flat from front to back (weight evenly distributed over the ball and the heel of your foot) and from side to side (equal pressure on the inside and the outside edges of your blade).

The first step to achieving great balance is learning the hockey-skating and hockey-playing positions. Whether with one hand on the stick or two hands on the stick, these positions are the starting point from which all of your moves on the ice will be made.

Proper Positioning

Start with your feet parallel and shoulder width apart, your knees bent and your back straight with your body leaning forward. You should be on a flat blade. Keep your shoulders square to the direction you will be traveling in and your head and core still.

If you are to engage with the puck you will need to be in the hockey-playing position with both of your hands properly on your stick (see page 22) and with your stick blade square on the ice. Keep your hands out a comfortable

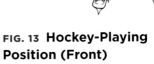

FIG. 13 Hockey-Playing Position (Front)
Bottom hand is in the center of your body and your top hand is in between the center of your body and your off-side hip. Your stick blade is flat on the ice and between your shoulders toward your proper side. Your feet are shoulder width apart pointing straight ahead.

FIG. 14 Hockey-Skating Position
Your back is straight with a forward body lean. Your head is up and still. Your knees are bent. You are on a flat blade. Your stick blade is square to the ice in between your shoulders (toward your off-side), and your top hand is away from your body in front of your off-side hip. Your feet are shoulder width apart pointing straight ahead.

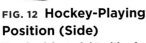

FIG. 12 Hockey-Playing Position (Side)
Your back is straight with a forward body lean. Your head is up and still. Your knees are bent. You are on a flat blade. Your stick blade is in front, square to the ice and between your shoulders toward your proper side. Hands are in the proper position, away from the body and your top- and bottom-hand grip are proper.

Drills to Develop Single-Leg Balance

Single-leg balance is a critical element of proper skating technique, as balancing on one skate allows you to drive, thrust and recover with your other skate (sometimes referred to as the "cycle of power"), so you can move efficiently around the ice. In many skating maneuvers, one skate stays on the ice for stability and glide while you work the other skate through a particular motion. A technical element players often overlook when developing a proper skating technique is the position of their stick. Proper use of your stick will assist your balance, as any time you only have one skate on the ice you can use your stick to help maintain your balance. By keeping your stick blade square on the ice and applying pressure through the shaft to the blade, your stick can act as another leg. This "third leg" allows you to keep your balance in any single-leg skating maneuver.

Thoughout these drills, maintain the hockey-skating position and focus on promoting glide by keeping your knees bent—especially over your glide skate.

Toe Taps
In the hockey-skating position, pick up one of your feet and move it laterally, just above the ice, toward your other foot and bring the insides of your skates together. Next, return the raised foot to its original position and then repeat with your other foot. As you become more comfortable, widen your step. Add puckhandling as you progress.

Step, Glide and Touch (Toe Taps in Motion)
Take a forward lateral step (not a stride) away from your body and put your weight over your stepping skate; bend the knee of this skate and glide. Pick up your other skate, keeping it close to the ice, and bring it to meet your gliding skate. Tap your skates together and then take a forward lateral step with the skate you just picked up. Continue to alternate skates, making sure to tap your skates in between steps. As you progress, widen your step. Try the same drill going backward.

Single-Leg Glide
Raise one skate off the ice and glide on your other skate. With your skate that is off the ice, execute leg and foot exercises. Alternate skates and try the drill both forward and backward. Here are a few exercise examples: you can rotate your hip and your ankle by pointing your toe out and in; you can move your skate away from your body and back toward your body; and you can bring your skate up and down while bending the knee of the skate you are gliding on to create a vertical weight transfer.

distance from your body with your arms slightly bent but not reaching (this will keep your stick blade square to the ice). Place your top hand between the center of your body and your off-side hip (right hip for a left-hander, left hip for a right-hander) and your bottom hand in the center of your body. Be sure to keep your hands forward —when viewed from the side, the elbow of your top hand should not extend behind your back. If your elbow is protruding behind you, your hands aren't forward enough.

If do not have the puck and aren't about to come in contact with it, you should be in the hockey-skating position with only your top hand on your stick. Keep your top hand forward and in front of your off-side hip so that your arm is slightly bent and your stick blade is square on the ice, in between your shoulders. In all skating maneuvers you should be able to control your stick and quickly move it into this position. Keep your same-side arm slightly bent, out from your hip and ready for action.

Skating Principles

Skating efficiently is the best and quickest way to improve your game. In order for you to understand how to become a better skater, you must embrace three important concepts that will affect your ability to perform on the ice: glide, drive and thrust.

Glide

Glide is the ability to "run" or coast your blades along the ice with as little friction as possible. Glide turns power into speed. It also allows you to create momentum during transitions.

Every skating maneuver has an element of glide. While you are skating, one of your feet will usually be gliding while the other is driving. Even when you are executing a power start or doing rapid cross-overs, the skate that is not driving is gliding, even if it is only doing so briefly. In other skating maneuvers where both of your feet continually stay on the ice, such as when you are skating forward or backward with both skates on the ice or when executing a tight turn, you are gliding with both skates while you are driving (for instance, when going backward the ball of your foot is thrusting while your heel is gliding). These moves cannot be performed efficiently without mastering how to glide.

You must be on a flat blade to maximize glide. Placing your

weight (hands, knees, etc.) on and out in front of a flat blade will enhance glide, effectively "drawing" you toward that weight. This is why you can increase the speed of your glide with a deep knee bend that is over the toe of your glide skate or by moving your hands into the proper position ahead of your glide skate. The more efficient your glide, the less power you need to exert to reach your desired speed on the ice.

Transferring your weight onto your glide skate will also increase the speed of your glide by putting weight ahead of your flat blade. When skating with both feet on the ice you can move quite quickly without actually "skating" simply by putting all of your weight on one skate and then transferring all of your weight onto your other skate, each time bending the knee of the leg that is receiving the transfer of weight. This movement demonstrates the impact that a transfer of weight has on glide.

Remember, in order to glide your skates must be on the ice! This is why great skaters keep their blades as close to the ice as possible, ensuring they are able to get their skates on the ice quickly and to keep them in contact with

the ice as much as possible. This is why you should avoid any training that teaches you to unnecessarily pick your feet up too high off the ice during skating maneuvers. The more your skates are on the ice, the more efficient a skater you can be.

Drive

Drive is one of two ways that you can develop power while skating. Drive means the action of your drive leg, such that the skate of that leg (the drive skate) pushes against the ice, exerting force that is transferred to your glide skate (the skate that is not pushing). Remember, once you are moving, when one skate drives, the other glides. The harder you drive, the more energy you will direct to your glide skate. Provided you are gliding efficiently, a powerful drive will translate into speed.

Thrust

Thrust is the second way to develop power while skating. Thrust is the additional power generated by the balls and the heels of the feet while driving. You produce thrust in your drive skate by extending and rotating your ankles, which manipulate the

ball or the heel of your drive skate. When timed properly, this directs a surge of power toward your glide skate adding to the power from the initial drive and increasing the speed of your glide skate. Ideally, extension of your ankle occurs at the same time as the extension of your drive leg.

During some maneuvers you can also generate thrust while you are gliding. For example, when skating forward with both skates continuously on the ice, you can generate thrust with your glide: your drive skate can glide on the ball of your foot and thrust with your heel while your other skate is gliding. Similarly, when skating backward with both skates continuously on the ice, your drive skate can drive with the ball of your foot but glide on your heel.

Great skaters can extend and rotate their ankles in almost any direction in order to generate the most thrust possible during any given skating maneuver. Timing is critical to maximize thrust and, consequently, maximize speed. Proper timing of the thrust together with proper weight transfer is what is commonly referred to as "rhythm" in skating. Rhythm has a huge effect on a player's ability to skate efficiently and to generate momentum during skating transitions.

When the ability to create thrust is combined with a strong drive and an efficient glide, a skater has an incredible ability to perform on the ice.

Cycle of Power

Jonathan Toews is using the forward stride to move himself up the ice. Toews' left foot is driving, and when his leg is fully extended he will thrust with an ankle extension off the inside edge of his blade at the ball of his foot. Toews is about to put his right foot back on the ice in order to glide. The power from the drive/thrust will be directed to the glide foot. Toews is leaning forward, which will allow him to add body weight to his glide.

3 Skating Techniques

Marty St. Louis executes a backward-to-forward transition. See page 56 for more on how to make a seamless backward-to-forward transition.

Forward Stride

You must be able to move forward in a straight line as fast as possible, with or without the puck. There are many game situations when straightaway speed without the puck is important: when racing for a loose puck, when chasing an opponent, when forechecking, when backchecking or when trying to get open for a pass. The fastest and most efficient way to move forward is by using the forward stride, striding (driving) with one leg and then the other, over and over. When one leg is striding, the other is gliding.

The Motion of the Drive Skate

Start in the hockey-skating position. With both skates parallel and under the center of your body, point your feet straight ahead. Make sure that the blades of both of your skates are flat, which will allow maximum glide on the glide skate and maximum push off the drive skate. With a deep knee bend, begin to rotate the toe of your drive skate out and away from your body. At the same time, push the entire inside edge of the blade of your drive skate into the ice and away from your glide skate. Do this using both the ball and the heel of your drive foot to produce a uniform push across the entire blade. The glide skate will move forward while you push the drive skate on the ice and extend your drive leg. When you push, you are rotating (opening) your hip and knee as you extend and straighten your leg.

You need to rotate your hip and knee enough so that the angle of the drive skate relative to your line of travel increases progressively, reaching a maximum of 90 degrees to your direction of travel at the end of your stride.

Remember, that as you drive, you are not only directing a surge of power toward your glide skate, you are also transferring your weight to the glide skate. At the start of a stride there is an initial transfer of weight to the glide skate, and more weight is progressively transferred to the glide skate as the stride continues. Transferring body weight to your glide skate, coupled with a balanced glide leg, allows you to be in the proper linear body position throughout your stride— your weight over your knee which is over the ball of your glide foot.

The Thrust of the Drive Skate
At the end of your stride, when your leg is *almost* fully extended and your drive skate is 90 degrees

to your line of travel, push off the ice. Start the push using your full blade and end the push by extending your ankle down into the ice, away from your body. The extension will give you an added thrust to your stride. Your ankle extension and final thrust should be off the inside edge of the ball of your foot. Remember to extend your leg completely as you finish your thrust.

Body Position Throughout the Stride
Throughout the stride, keep your head and torso as still as possible. Keep your shoulders square to your line of travel and your back straight as you lean your body forward. At all times, your glide skate should remain in a straight line and on a flat blade in line with your direction of travel. Use a deep knee bend to keep your body weight forward, over your glide skate. The knee of your glide leg and the hand of your glide arm should be over the toe of your glide skate.

Your glide-side arm should swing forward (but not across your body) as you drive.

Being in the proper body position throughout your stride allows you to use the large muscle groups in your body, such as your back and quadriceps, to increase the strength of your drive throughout your stride.

Recovery of the Drive Leg
After you make the final thrust off the ball of your drive foot, you must bring it back (recover) to the glide position, as your glide foot will then become your drive foot. You must do this as quickly as possible so your other skate can begin to stride and thus keep you moving forward as quickly as possible. The speed of your recovery is crucial to executing the most strides in the shortest amount of time. Recover as quickly as possible by fully transferring your weight to your glide skate during the drive motion. As well, keep your drive skate up off the ice, but as close to the ice as possible, after the final thrust and during the recovery. Your single-leg balance is extremely important throughout the stride, as it allows you to fully transfer your weight, which enables maximum glide and drive for the quickest recovery.

The Cycle of Power
Once you recover your drive foot and drive with your glide foot you will have completed one full drive

Derick Brassard

1. Left shoulder is dropped, and not square to the direction of travel, because Brassard is placing his bottom hand on the stick as he is about to engage with the puck. Brassard's top hand is in perfect position, away from his body.

2. Skate is in the middle of the drive, rotated out 90 degrees from the direction of travel, pushing uniformly across the entire blade. As the drive continues, Brassard will thrust from the ball of his foot and increase his speed by extending his ankle down, forcing his blade further into the ice.

3. Left skate is recovering from a drive. Brassard keeps his recovering skate low to the ice so that he can get it in a gliding position as soon as possible.

FIG. 15 Start
Feet underneath your body on flat blades increases the weight you can contribute to your drive.

FIG. 16 Initial Push
Initial drive foot is turned out to begin your stride and knees are bent to power your drive. Push uniformly across the entire blade.

FIG. 17 Drive
Continue the uniform push across the entire blade while you shift to using your inside edge exclusively, while at the same time rocking from your heel to the ball of your foot for the final thrust.

cycle. Repeat the entire process until you have reached your goal, whether it be catching a player or breaking for open ice.

Tips for Speed

Proper positioning and good conditioning of your quads, hamstrings and core will help you attain speed, as will the following tips:

* Skate efficiently: keep your head and torso still and your shoulders square.
* Glide is as important as power. Glide on a flat blade and with a deep knee bend.
* If there is no immediate chance of getting the puck while striding, only your top hand should be on your stick.
* If you are looking for a pass or are about to enter a battle for the puck, both of your hands should

Perfect Glide
Brad Boyes has finished thrusting with his left skate and is gliding beautifully on his right skate. The key to Boyes' glide is a horizontally and vertically flat blade (efficient transfer of drive power), a good knee bend with body weight over and ahead of his glide skate (weight increases glide) and keeping square to the direction of travel (allowing the glide skate to point straight).

FIG. 18 Thrust
From the ball of your foot, push hard down into the ice. For extra speed extend your ankle down and away from your direction of travel, forcing your blade into the ice.

FIG. 19 Glide to Stride
Throughout the entire stride (Fig. 15–18), keep your glide foot flat with your weight ahead of your blade to keep you traveling straight. As your drive foot recovers, begin striding with your glide foot — progressively rotating it out 90 degrees from your direction of travel — to set up your drive.

be on your stick. Do not move your hands and stick side to side; rather, move them back to front in sequence with your stride. Do not let your arms cross the centerline of your body.

＊ Keep the blade of your stick square to the ice and between your shoulders.

The Secret to Going Even Faster

You can add another gear to your forward stride by extending your ankle at the end of each stride. When your drive leg is almost fully extended, with the heel of your skate blade still on the ice and your foot 90 degrees to your line of travel, push down and off the ice using your heel. Next, rock on your drive skate blade from your heel to the ball of your foot, and at

the same time extend your ankle down and away from your line of travel. This drives the ball of your foot down into the ice and creates thrust, which will propel you quickly forward. Rocking from the heel to the ball of the foot is much the same technique basketball players and high jumpers use to spring up and sprinters use to run fast. The heel rocking to the ball of the foot coupled with the increased push off the ball of the foot by extending the ankle greatly increases the force of the final push at the end of each stride.

Notes

If your arm crosses your centerline at the end of your stride, it will force the heel of your skate off the ice, and you will not be able to use it to push and rock onto the ball of your foot. This will considerably reduce the thrust you will be able to generate. Also, players who skate with both hands on their stick and move their hands laterally across their body are not able to use an ankle extension effectively; remember to move your hands in sequence with your stride, back to front. Finally, it takes great single-leg balance and timing to complete an ankle extension and not reduce the speed of your drive leg's recovery. It is rare for younger players to be able to master this technique, but mastering it can give you an edge over an opponent on a straightaway. It is very important that your skates are flexible enough to allow you to extend your ankles.

Forward Glide

You need to be able to generate forward speed with both of your skates on the ice. There are many situations during a game when this is important. Defensively, when containing and possibly contacting a player, having both skates on the ice allows you to maintain your body position while angling toward the offensive player, and it gives you stability just before contact. Offensively, if you are in a good position but want to move forward, such as when you are trailing a play or are in the high slot and in a good shooting position, you will want to generate forward speed while gliding. Also, every time you do a tight turn you are moving forward while keeping both of your skates on the ice.

Beginning to Glide

To develop maximum speed while gliding (from a position where you are already moving or a standing start), you must be in the hockey-skating position and on a flat blade with a deep knee bend. To glide efficiently, equally distribute your weight over your heels and the balls of your feet. To generate extra speed in this position, transfer your weight back and forth, completely over one skate and then over your other skate. This is a lateral (or horizontal) weight transfer. Moving your body weight up and down by bending and straightening your knees (vertical weight transfer) will also add speed.

In this position you can "stride" by alternately bringing one skate underneath you, touching it to your other skate and then pushing it in a stride motion away from your body with a full leg extension before

Mike Ribeiro

1 Knee is bent and leg is "striding" while not leaving the ice. Ribeiro is executing a heel push with the inside edge of his left skate (the drive skate), while horizontally transferring his body weight to his right side.

2 As Ribeiro shifts his body weight right, he bends his knee to put his body weight over and ahead of his right skate blade. His left blade will transfer from being on its inside edge to being flat in order to glide. Once the transfer is complete and his left blade is completely flat, Ribeiro will "stride" with his right leg before transferring his weight back to his left side.

recovering it back underneath you. Always keep your skates on the ice and always stay on a flat blade on your glide skate while executing this stride. It is also important that all of your power goes forward and in a straight line. While your drive skate is striding, your glide skate must be in a straight line.

The Power of the Heel Push

When you are moving forward with both skates on the ice, you can achieve maximum speed by generating thrust with a heel push: driving the inside edge of the heel of your skate into the ice and away from your body while gliding on a flat blade (this looks like a half-moon, or the letter "C"). The strength of your heel push will depend on the level of acceleration you require. The timing of your heel push is also critical. You must push when your drive skate is underneath you, or close to that position, ensuring that your body weight is over your drive skate at the time of your thrust.

To develop maximum speed, remember to drive with the heel of your drive skate while continuing to glide with a flat blade on the ball of your foot on your drive skate (while at the same time gliding on your other skate). If you put too much weight on your heels you will decrease your glide. This can prevent you from executing a glide turn (like a tight turn, see page 62) or from generating speed on a straightaway.

Heel Push Drill

The goal of this drill is to skate circles around a stick lying on the ice by only using heel pushes and gliding. To start, lay your stick on the ice and enter the hockey-skating position with your skates together and parallel to your stick. Turn the toe of the skate farthest from your stick out 90 degrees.

This skate is your outside skate, and in this drill your outside skate is always your drive skate. While always keeping your drive skate on the ice, drive forward by pushing the inside edge of your heel into the ice. Continue to extend the leg of your drive foot away from your inside skate (your glide skate). Recover by bringing your drive skate back underneath you to touch your glide skate, and remember to keep both skates on the ice at all times (your inside skate should always be gliding). When striding, your inside arm should point at your stick. Continue traveling around your stick by repeating the process, ensuring that you glide on a flat blade with both skates while you push. Stop and change directions to practice driving with the other foot. In this drill, your right skate will move you counterclockwise, and your left will move you clockwise. This exercise will teach you the importance of timing your thrust and fully extending your drive leg after your thrust.

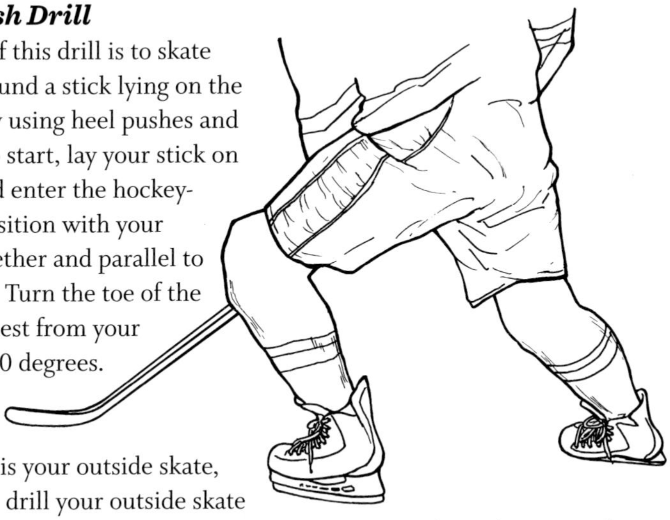

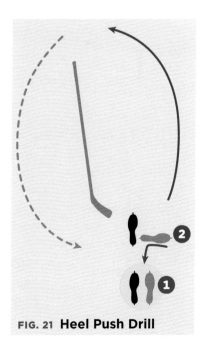

FIG. 20 Heel Push Extension and Recovery
Your drive leg is fully extended with your blade flat, front to back, when you end your drive. Keep your glide skate in a straight line underneath your body throughout the entire heel push and extension. This will maximize your glide and help you to avoid "weaving" back and fourth.

FIG. 21 Heel Push Drill

Forward Cross-Overs

You can generate a lot of forward speed by using cross-overs: bringing your outside skate over your inside skate while driving forward and laterally with both skates. You can use this technique from a stationary start; when moving forward in a turn or circle that is not tight, such as when driving to the net; when accelerating out of a tight turn; and when moving forward and laterally up the ice on an angle.

Drive with Both Skates

To start the cross-over motion, thrust from the inside edge of your outside skate at the ball of your foot as you pick this skate up to cross it over your inside skate. Quickly follow this with a cross-under: rotate the ankle of your inside skate and thrust underneath your cross-over skate from the outside edge of your blade at the pad of your foot. Extend your ankle (as your leg reaches the end of its drive) to drive the pad of your foot down into the ice to generate more thrust.

When doing cross-overs, emphasize the drive with short, quick strokes. Extend each of your legs at the end of their drives (especially when coming out of a turn).

The lower your skates stay to the ice throughout the cross-over, the quicker your recovery, the stronger your drive and the more time your blades will be on the ice to thrust. With cross-overs you want both skates to be driving at all times, and you want to move your skates so they cross closely together underneath you. This allows you to use as much of your body weight as possible to assist your thrust.

Shea Weber

1 Top hand is moved into the body (but out from the hip) and shoulders are square to the direction of travel. Stick blade is in line with the trajectory of the turn. If Weber were turning on a sharper angle, his top hand would come across his body toward the elbow of his bottom arm.

2 The cross-over skate (outside skate) is kept very close to the ice while crossing over top of the inside skate to allow for an efficient, quick recovery and speedy repetition of the stride.

3 The cross-under skate (inside skate) is driving underneath the cross-over skate, thrusting from the outside edge of the blade at the pad of the foot. As Weber continues his cross-under he will extend his leg (like in Fig. 23) and will then extend his ankle to drive the pad of his foot down into the ice to generate more thrust.

4 Knees are bent, allowing Weber to vertically transfer weight into the cross-over and cross-under, maximizing his drive and ensuring as much blade as possible is on the ice for his cross-over and cross-under thrust.

FIG. 22 Crossing Over
Lean into your turn and with the inside edge of your cross-over skate at the ball of your foot. Keep it as close as possible to the ice and the skate you are crossing over.

Rhythm Adds Speed

You will generate more speed with your cross-overs when you vertically transfer your weight by bending your knees in rhythm with your drive and leg extension. This is because bending your knees adds body weight to your drive and allows you to get more of your skate blades on the ice, increasing your thrust; players call this "bounce." The key to bounce is to vertically transfer your weight but still keep your skates on or close to the ice. You can maximize your drive by timing your ankle extension to coincide with the end of your leg extension.

Stick Position

Where you put your stick always dictates the position of your hands and body; cross-overs are no different. The blade of your stick should always be between your shoulders, which should be square to your line of travel. Therefore, if you are doing cross-overs around a circle on the ice, you are looking into the circle but the blade of your stick should be on the circle itself and in front of you, *not* pointed toward the face-off dot. To place the blade of your stick in this position when crossing over to your backhand, move your top hand away from your body. When crossing over to your forehand, move your top hand into, and possibly across, your body. This will add glide and speed to your crossovers and will help you to protect the puck. Both these positions are very similar to the positions you use when doing tight turns (see page 62).

FIG. 23 Crossing Under
As your outside skate is crossing over, rotate your ankle on your inside skate so that you are using the outside edge of that skate, and push, with the pad of your foot, underneath the skate that is crossing over. Recover this foot quickly toward the center of the turn so that you can cross under again.

Backward Stride

All players must be able to skate backward with balance and speed. If you are playing defense and can match the speed of attacking forwards when skating backward, you can maintain proper positioning. Forwards often skate backward during a game, especially when moving into the proper shooting position, when assuming a proper position while forechecking or when defending after replacing a pinching player on defense. The skating principles that apply to the forward glide (see page 36) also apply to the backward stride. The exception is that your thrust now comes from the balls of your feet as opposed to your heels.

Brian Rafalski

1. Head is up and shoulders are square, opposite to the direction of travel; back is straight with a forward lean.

2. Hands are in the hockey-skating position. Knee of glide leg is well bent to keep weight over the glide skate for better glide and stability.

3. Glide skate is traveling straight and on a flat blade for most efficient glide.

4. Striding leg is almost fully extended while doing a "C" cut, with the heel and ball of the foot still in contact with the ice. Rafalski will finish his drive without picking up the heel of his drive skate by applying pressure with the ball of his foot through an ankle extension.

The Drive

Start in the hockey-skating position with your feet together and parallel. Make sure to keep a deep knee bend and your back straight with your heels down on the ice. Turn the toe of one of your feet inward, this will be the foot you first drive off. Thrust yourself backward with your turned foot, from the inside edge of your blade at the ball of that foot. This stride is like the stride of the heel push (only backward—see page 37) and should create a half-moon or the letter "C." Put as much pressure as possible onto the ball of your foot for the drive, particularly at the start of your stride.

The Stride

After your drive, continue to extend your stride leg fully out in front of you. However, you'll notice that the slower you are traveling the wider your stride will be. As you travel faster the thrusts from the balls of your feet will become straighter and less out and away from your body. Be sure to keep your glide leg traveling in a straight line underneath you, with the heel of your glide foot down. This allows you to take advantage of your weight, which will help you promote glide. At the end of your stroke, recover your stride foot and bring it back underneath you, beside and touching your glide foot. This is called "push and touch." It ensures that you get a full stride and that, before your glide foot begins its stride, your drive foot has come back and is ready to glide. In the backward stride, both skates stay on the ice at all times. You can use vertical and horizontal transfers of weight, just as you would use during the forward glide and forward stride.

Notes

It is important to focus all of your power on moving backward as fast as possible in a straight line. When your drive skate is going through the stride motion, your glide skate must be in a straight line under you and your shoulders must be square, so that you are facing opposite your direction of travel. This ensures that you will move straight backward rather than turning from side to side with every stride.

FIG. 24 **The Drive**
Toe is turned inward and your blade is flat on the ice. Push backward from the inside edge of your blade at the ball of your drive foot. Do not pick up your heel: your push should be a full-blade thrust with emphasis on the ball of your foot. By keeping your heel on the ice you are gliding on your heel while you are thrusting, making you go faster.

The most common mistake players make when striding backward is lifting their heels off the ice. This action makes you lose the crucial heel glide that promotes speed and keeps you headed straight backward. Other common mistakes are not extending the drive leg fully, which maximizes thrust, and not bringing the feet together underneath the body between strides, which maximizes the body weight on the glide.

Push and Touch

Brian Rafalski matches the speed of rushing winger Corey Perry while skating backward. Rafalski is performing "push and touch." Touching your feet together underneath your body ensures a full extension of the stride and means that when your drive skate becomes your glide skate, it will be underneath your body and you will be using your weight to maximize glide.

FIG. 25 End of the Stride

Continue your initial push by extending your drive skate (with a flat blade) out in front of your body. For added speed before you recover your stride leg, extend your ankle forward at the end of your stride and thrust the ball of your foot into the ice. Use the rocking method you learned in the forward stride (page 32). Pumping your arm and pointing it in tandem with your striding leg will increase your speed.

The Secret to Extreme Speed on a Backward Stride

If you want to maximize your backward speed, you must learn to extend your ankles to create thrust. Start flexing your ankle when your feet are together, at the start of your stride. This ankle extension will continue through to the end of the stride. At the start of each stride, the pressure should be down and out through the ball of your foot, opposite your direction of travel. This push is commonly called a "C" cut. However, as you gain speed the thrusts from the balls of your feet will become straighter and less out and away from your body. The key to maximizing the thrust from the ball of your foot is to extend your ankle down into the ice and push back away from your body opposite to your direction of travel.

Backward Cross-Under

The ability to turn is important whether you are skating forward or backward. Performing a backward cross-under allows you to accelerate while turning backward, which can help you get into a proper defensive position quickly and, offensively, get open for shots and passes. You can use the cross-under technique during many other skating maneuvers, such as backward skating, backward lateral skating and transition skating, to add speed and acceleration to your game.

Not a Cross-Over

This technique is not a cross-over—it is a cross-under. Contrary to the commonly held view, and unlike when turning forward, you cross your feet under, not over, when turning backward. With cross-unders, your glide skate (outside skate) stays on the ice at all times to maximize glide and stability. Even your driving skate stays close to the ice, since you don't need to pick it up and move it over your gliding skate, making this a very efficient skating maneuver.

Setting Up

As you are skating backward in the hockey-skating position, lean your body in toward the inside of the turn you wish to take. Keep your shoulders square and turn your head toward the inside of the turn so you can see where you are going. If you have the puck, or it is in immediate play, skate with two hands on your stick. Otherwise, skate with only your top hand on your stick.

Ready to Cross-Under
Barret Jackman begins a backward turn by pushing off the inside edge of his outside (right) skate at the ball of his foot. He is in the process of drawing the ice with his inside (left) skate using a flat blade. Jackman will push his inside skate toward and underneath his outside skate to execute a cross-under stride. He will rotate and extend his inside ankle, pushing the outside edge of his blade at the pad of his foot down and into the ice, to thrust at the end of his cross-under.

Reach and Pull

Your inside skate should drive and do all of the work. Your outside skate should glide and provide stability. Begin the cross-under stride by reaching your inside skate into the turn, away from your body, and "grabbing" the ice with the full length of the blade. Next, "pull" the ice you just grabbed toward you with the inside edge of your inside skate. This is commonly referred to as "reach and pull."

Push and Thrust

As your inside skate pulls progressively closer to your outside skate, you need to cross it underneath your body and behind the heel of your outside skate to push and thrust, completing the stride. To do this, bend the knee of your inside leg progressively so the full blade of your inside skate can remain on the ice to push. As well, rotate your inside ankle so, as your blade drives underneath you and behind the heel of your outside skate, your skate will transition from the inside edge to horizontally flat then to the outside edge.

As you cross your inside skate under you, you should be pushing with the outside edge of your blade. As you continue to push past the heel of your glide skate you will need to extend your leg and thrust. Use the pad of your foot to propel

the thrust at the end of your drive and extend your ankle to maximize this thrust.

Recovery

Right after the final thrust, start your recovery by quickly moving your drive skate back to a position

Kimmo Timonen
Backward Lateral Skating with a Cross-Under

1 Head is up and looking at attacker. Shoulders are square to attacker and arms are in proper position. Defending the rush with an extended reach causes slight lean on body, as does the attacker's forward lateral movement, causing Timonen to respond with a backward lateral defensive movement.

2 Right foot is recovering from a drive underneath the body during a cross-under. Note how the foot is low to the ice and both knees are well bent. Left foot is on a slight angle due to the nature of the attack, but is flat from front to back, ensuring a good glide while he is moving backward laterally.

where it can "reach and pull" again. You are stepping with your skate toward the inside of the turn. When recovering, try to keep your drive skate as close as you can to the ice. Remember, you are repeating the stride with the same leg (the inside leg).

FIG. 26 Cross-Under
Glide skate remains flat while your drive skate crosses underneath and behind the heel of your glide skate. Finish the drive with a thrust from the outside edge of your skate blade at the ball of your foot. For extra power extend your ankle down, forcing your blade into the ice.

The Glide Skate

Your outside skate (your glide skate) remains on the ice at all times throughout the reach and pull, the push and thrust and the recovery. To maximize the glide on this skate, make sure you stay on a flat blade. Proper body position will ensure that your weight is evenly distributed on this skate and you are on a flat blade. Both your drive leg (your inside leg) and glide leg (your outside leg) require a deep knee bend; this promotes glide as well as balance and drive. Your glide skate must glide efficiently in order for you to maximize the acceleration you have while turning backward.

Backward Lateral Skating

When defending against an attacking player, you need to be able to move backward laterally while keeping square to the attacking player. Offensively, changing angles by moving backward laterally with the puck can help you create shooting or passing lanes; when you don't have the puck, moving backward laterally allows you to move into a shooting or passing lane, where you can receive the puck.

With this technique, having quick feet really pays off. Skating backward laterally is very much like executing a backward cross-under, except you aren't leaning into a turn or reaching and pulling as far or as aggressively. However, the footwork required for backward lateral skating is essentially the same as a backward cross-under: you still reach and pull with your inside drive skate as your outside skate glides. The key difference is that you are taking shorter strides with your drive skate and doing them at a faster rate.

Method
Before striding you need to be moving backward on the angle you wish to travel in. Be in the hockey-skating position, with a good knee bend and your shoulders square. To move laterally backward, reach away from your body with your drive skate (in the direction you wish to move), grab some ice and draw your drive skate toward your glide skate — just as you do when executing a backward cross-under. Finish the drive by pushing behind and underneath with the outside edge of your glide skate. This drive does not need to be as pronounced and extended as when doing a cross-under, and the main drive (thrust) should come from the pad of your foot as you extend you ankle down, toward the ice. The whole time your outside skate should stay on the ice as you glide backward on it. This ensures that you will be moving backward while you are still moving laterally.

Repeating the drive cycle as quickly as possible is essential to move quickly while skating backward laterally. The strokes need to be kept short, and you must quickly recover your drive skate after each stroke. This is why, compared to a cross-under, the movement requires less reach at the outset of the drive and less extension at the conclusion of the stride.

The keys to speed when skating backward laterally are: quick feet to rapidly draw the ice, vertical weight transfers and efficient ankle extensions for quick recovery.

Lateral Slides and Stopping

Every player needs to be able to stop, but it is not often that you will come to a complete stop during a game. Sometimes you will want to go to a certain place on the ice and stay there temporarily. Other times stopping is the most efficient way for you to reverse your direction, and you may need to stop if you have limited room to maneuver.

The Lateral Slide

The lateral slide is a technique that not only precedes a stop, it is also used during some transitions—such as going forward to backward and going forward to forward—in order to preserve speed. You can also use it as a technique on its own to move laterally with or without the puck.

A lateral slide is preformed anytime both your feet are turned 90 degrees to your direction of travel while your momentum carries you in your original direction. Sometimes this is for a very brief moment, such as in a forward-to-forward transition (see page 58), and other times the slide is more pronounced, such as a two-foot stop. The hardest skill to learn is how to do a lateral slide over a longer distance without stopping, with knees bent and ready to drive.

Begin a lateral slide by transitioning from a forward glide (having both of your feet coasting parallel on the ice with your toes pointing in the direction you are traveling in) to having both your feet and your body turned 90 degrees to your direction of travel. To do this, straighten your legs to lift your weight off your skates and exit the forward glide; the decreased pressure on your blades allows you to turn both your feet and your body against your direction of travel. Once turned do not apply any pressure on your skates, as this will make you stop. Instead, keep your legs straight and continue being light on your blades. It is important that both skate blades remain flat.

The less pressure you put on your blades, the less resistance you'll encounter and the more you will slide. You will eventually stop when the pressure of your blades causes enough drag to bring your lateral slide to an end. On a fresh sheet of ice, a proper lateral slide will leave two parallel scrape marks that look like jet streams and that end together at the center of your back skate's blade. As you become more adept at sliding laterally, practice bending your knees (vertical weight transfers) while you slide. A bent-knee lateral slide is the best way to accelerate out of a transition, as your legs must be bent at the end of your slide to maximize your initial drive.

Two-Foot Stop

Stopping on two skates requires a lateral slide on both blades with a gradual application of pressure until the drag created by the blades on the ice makes you stop.

Start the stop motion from a forward glide and transfer to a lateral slide with both of your feet. Once in the slide, put your body weight onto your skates by bending your knees (vertical weight transfer). The deeper you bend your knees, the more pressure you apply to your blades; the quicker you bend your knees, the quicker that pressure is applied. This allows you to control when and where the stop is made. As your stop advances, lean further away from your direction of travel and increase the pressure on the inside edge of your front skate and the outside edge of your back skate.

You will need speed to do this adequately. Remember to keep your skates close together in the slide to effectively use your edges when you stop. As you continue to practice you'll get more comfortable using the outside edge of your back skate. You should progress to the point where you are executing two-foot stops with your feet almost touching.

Henrik Zetterberg

1 Body leans away from the direction of travel to increase pressure on the inside edge of the front skate and the outside edge of the back skate, turning the lateral slide into a two-foot stop; shoulders and head remain square to the direction the skates are pointing.

2 Vertical weight transfers (knee bends) are used to provide pressure on the skate blades to help execute the two-foot stop.

3 Feet are staggered slightly to help provide stability.

4 Top hand is away from the body when handling the puck on the backhand side of the blade, and is rotated to cup the puck.

47

As you master the lateral slide, you will be able to determine how long to glide before rotating your body and how long to slide laterally before stopping. The glide can be very short as the transition from skating to stopping can be very quick.

You can also perform a two-foot stop without rotating your upper body. Instead, keep your shoulders square to your direction of travel by only turning from the waist down when stopping. You'll want to stop this way to keep facing the play, especially if you are looking for a pass or a rebound.

Progressive Stop Drill

To stop you must learn to put pressure on the ice laterally using the entire blade of your skate (or skates, if you are executing a two-foot stop). To practice this skill, set one knee on the ice and place the skate of your other leg beside this knee. With the skate blade beside your knee and flat on the ice, push your foot laterally across the ice, away from your body. Apply pressure across your entire blade and keep your skate as straight as possible; you are trying to make snow by scraping the top layer off the ice.

Next, repeat the same exercise, but as you push the scraping foot away from your body, start to angle the skate away from your body as well, increasingly using the inside edge. Be sure to perform each step with each foot. Next, repeat the two steps while standing. Finally, add movement by driving off of one skate and sliding laterally with the other.

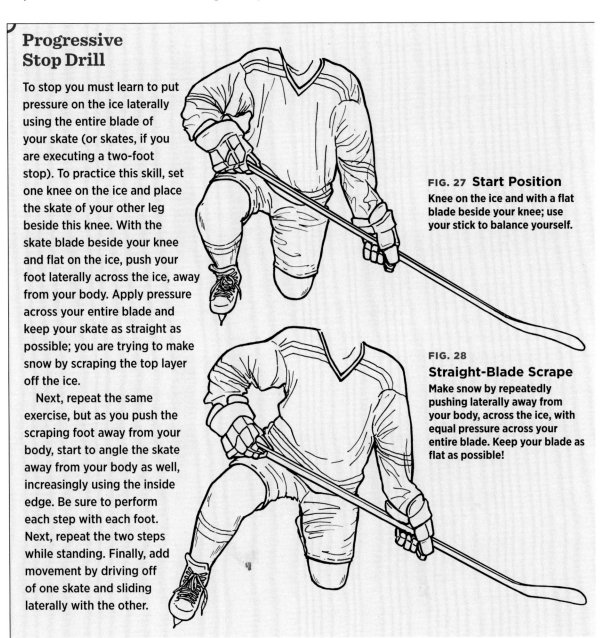

FIG. 27 Start Position
Knee on the ice and with a flat blade beside your knee; use your stick to balance yourself.

FIG. 28

Straight-Blade Scrape
Make snow by repeatedly pushing laterally away from your body, across the ice, with equal pressure across your entire blade. Keep your blade as flat as possible!

Forward Power Start

Accelerating quickly from a stop or off a forward glide can give you a huge advantage when racing to loose pucks and breaking away from checkers. A lot of hockey happens in "small area" game situations, such as forechecking and puck possession in the offensive zone; quickness in these areas can be even more important than overall speed.

Two Starts, Three Methods

There are two types of starts: the V-start (or heels-in start) and the cross-over start.

For the V-start, line up square to your desired direction of travel, with your heels in and together and your toes pointing out. You should have a deep knee bend (lower than you would for normal forward striding) with a forward lean, and your heels should be underneath you so you can use your body weight to help maximize the pressure on your blades. Start by driving off the inside edge of one skate with a thrust from the ball of your foot. For a cross-over start, begin with your feet parallel and your skates and body at 90 degrees to your desired direction of travel. Again, a knee bend deeper than a standard striding knee bend is needed, and your weight should be evenly distributed along your blades. Lead with your back foot and begin with one cross-over—thrust from the ball of your foot. Follow immediately with a

Chris Kelly

1. Shoulders are square to the direction of travel and arms are in the hockey-playing position, holding the stick properly so as to cup the puck.

2. Legs are close together and close to the ice for a compact initial cross-over start, allowing for rapid stride recovery.

3. Back foot has just launched—from the ball of the foot on the inside edge of the skate blade—and is crossing over the front foot. Front foot is crossing under the back foot and is about to thrust from the pad of the foot on the outside edge of the skate blade.

front foot cross-under as your back foot crosses over, pushing from the pad of your foot on the outside edge of your cross-under skate. As you move through the cross-over and cross-under, rotate your upper body until you are square to your desired direction of travel and ready to stride forward.

With both methods, there are three different techniques you can use to get going:

1 Immediately take a full stride;
2 run on the balls of your feet for three steps and then take a full stride;
3 run on the balls of your feet for two to three quick steps and then start striding, beginning with short strides and increasing to full strides.

Some players have great success with an immediate full stride ,provided they are able to quickly and fully recover; this works well for some smaller or lighter players. Other players have greater success with three running steps before taking a full stride. The ideal method for most players is the third technique, as it combines a quick running start with shorter initial strides to ensure the drive leg recovers quickly. However, you should try all three techniques and both methods to see which suits you best.

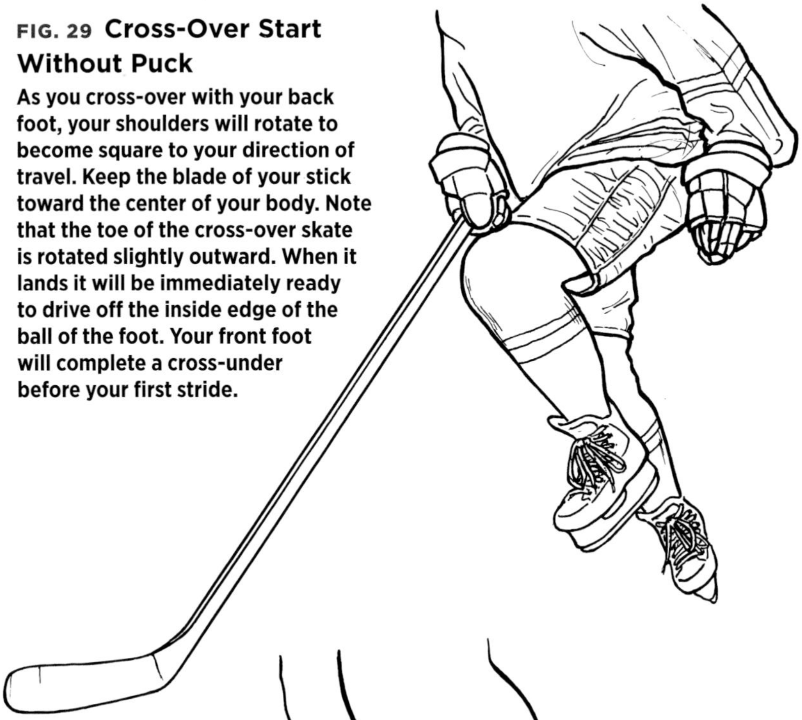

Notes

It is crucial that you make the driving steps from the inside edge of your blades at the balls of your feet, not your toes. This ensures that your toes are rotated out as

FIG. 29 Cross-Over Start Without Puck
As you cross-over with your back foot, your shoulders will rotate to become square to your direction of travel. Keep the blade of your stick toward the center of your body. Note that the toe of the cross-over skate is rotated slightly outward. When it lands it will be immediately ready to drive off the inside edge of the ball of the foot. Your front foot will complete a cross-under before your first stride.

FIG. 30 Quick Step
After your initial stride, recover your blades as close to the ice as you can and keep the toe of your thrusting foot rotated out as far as possible so that you can thrust from the inside edge of your blade at the ball of your foot. This is also what the first thrust of a V-start should look like.

far as possible, making your skates close to 90 degrees to your line of travel and giving you more blade and a better angle to push off of. When running or using short strides, do not extend you ankles, as this delays the recovery of your drive foot. Once you start taking full strides, you should extend your ankles to add thrust at the end of each stride.

Move your arms forward in your direction of travel. While running or doing short strides, moving your arms in the proper skating motion will help you accelerate.

Quickly recovering your feet is a key ingredient to a quick start. You must move your feet as quickly as possible and still maintain great technique to ensure an explosive start.

Backward Power Start

Getting a fast, straight backward start can be the difference between stopping a play or allowing an odd player rush or, even worse, a breakaway. It can also help you quickly get open for a shot or a pass.

From Start to Cross-Over

To power start backward, get in the hockey-skating position and rotate your lower body so that your skates are parallel and 90 degrees to your intended direction. Transfer your weight to your front skate—this will become your drive skate. With a deep knee bend, push off your drive skate and extend your leg in front of you. With pressure on your inside edge, rock from the heel to the ball of your foot and extend your ankle away from you and down into the ice; thrust straight backward off your inside edge at the ball of your foot.

After you thrust straight backward, lift your drive skate off the ice and cross it over your glide skate, which will have pivoted underneath you so that your heel is pointing in your intended direction of travel and you are gliding straight backward.

Cross-Under and Stride

As soon as your drive skate lands from your cross-over, execute a cross-under with your glide skate. Push straight back with the outside edge of your skate at the pad of your foot and extend your leg behind the heel of your cross-over skate. As your leg is fully extended, push your ankle down toward the ice to thrust off the outside edge of

FIG. 31 Start Position
Weight is transferred to your front foot, resulting in a deep knee bend. Drive backward off the inside edge of your entire blade, rocking from the heel of your foot to the ball of your foot for extra thrust.

FIG. 32 Leg Extension from the Start
Leg is extended so that you drive straight back. The ankle is extended down and away from you, driving the inside edge of your blade at the ball of your foot into the ice.

FIG. 33 Cross-Over
Recover your drive skate in toward your body and cross it over your gliding skate, which will have pivoted so that your heel is pointing toward your intended direction of travel.

FIG. 34 Cross-Under
Your original drive skate is the glide skate during your cross-under. Extend your cross-under leg behind the heel of your glide skate. Rotate and extend your ankle on your cross-under skate to drive from the outside edge at the pad of your foot. Recover this skate underneath your body and beside your glide skate, and tap the insides of your skates together before striding with your original drive skate.

your blade at the pad of your foot. During your cross-under, glide backward on your cross-over skate.

Quickly recover your cross-under skate to a position underneath your body and beside your glide skate, and tap the insides of your skates together (like you do in a push and touch—see page 42). Stride backward with the entire blade of your original drive skate, extending your leg fully out in front of you. Extend your ankle and thrust into the ice off the inside edge of this skate at the ball of your foot. Continue alternating drive legs as you stride backward.

Notes

The technique of crossing over, then crossing under and then striding backward is important because this chain of movement will keep you on as straight a line as possible through the backward power start and make the sequence as efficient as possible.

This is a very complex maneuver. To help you complete the transition and correctly position your skates, you can think, "over, under, stride" in relation to your movements and "inside, outside, inside" in relation to the edge-work of your skates. It is also important to touch your skates together under you after you complete the cross-under, as this will ensure that your first backward stride is a full one.

Chris Pronger

1. Shoulders and torso are square, opposite to the direction of travel. Stick blade remains in the middle of the body. Arms pump to help propel the backward power start.

2. Left leg (the original drive leg) has pushed off and has just finished the cross-over portion of the backward power start. This skate will now glide while the right skate crosses under. Pronger's deep knee bend and his flat blade will help him glide backward in a straight line with speed.

3. Right foot is completing the cross-under with a thrust from the outside edge, at the pad of the foot. Pronger rotates his ankle to get as much of the outside edge on the ice as possible. Once this foot recovers, Pronger will stride with his left foot.

Forward-to-Backward Transition

If there is one thing that is constant in hockey, it is transition! You need to be able to move up the ice and back while always facing the play. There are numerous situations where a seamless transition from skating forward in one direction to skating backward in the opposite direction while staying square to the original direction of travel is needed, such as when the defense follows a play up the ice and there is a turnover or when a forward driving to the net gets in too deep and wants to move back into a better position while still facing the puck.

Duncan Keith

1 Keith is at the end of his lateral slide in his transition from gliding forward to striding backward while continuously facing the play. Next, Keith will pivot his back skate so that the heel of this skate will face his desired direction of travel. Keith will then apply pressure to his front skate in order to perform a backward power start.

2 During his lateral slide, Keith's shoulders, hips and torso rotated away from the play. He has turned his head to face the play, and as he comes out of the lateral slide and into his backward power start, he will rotate his body to be square to the play and will drive straight backward.

Method One: Slide to Backward Power Start

Start a forward-to-backward transition by skating forward then making a forward lateral slide (see page 46). The lateral slide is then combined with a backward power start (see page 51). The slide ensures that some of your forward speed is maintained as you change direction, giving you momentum going into your power start. The backward power start (started while still in the slide motion) allows you to move backward quickly and efficiently.

When you reach the point of your slide where you want to start going backward, bend the knee of your front leg (which is leading your lateral slide) and transfer your weight onto your front skate. As your weight comes off your back skate, pivot it so that the heel of your back skate is toward the direction you want to travel backward. Next, initiate a backward power start with your front skate.

Do not forget—the backward power start method is: one cross-over, one cross-under, feet brought together and a backward stride. It is imperative that your thrust and ankle extension for both the power start and the cross-under are straight back and away from your direction of travel to keep you on as straight a line as possible and to make the transition as efficient as possible.

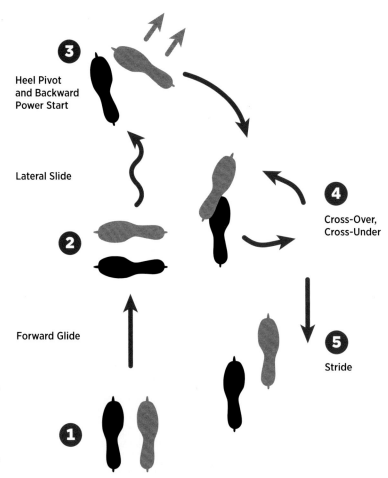

3 Heel Pivot and Backward Power Start

Lateral Slide

2

Forward Glide

1

4 Cross-Over, Cross-Under

5 Stride

FIG. 35 Method One: Slide to Backward Power Start

Method Two: The Pivot

If you are not advancing straight up the ice but are moving forward on an angle and don't need to maintain a straight line in your transition from forward to backward, you can use the forward-to-backward pivot to maintain speed through your transition.

As you are moving up the ice on an angle, glide forward with your skates shoulder width apart, parallel and facing forward. Next, raise your weight off your skates by straightening your legs, and pivot the heels of your skates so they point in your new direction of travel. At the same time, bend your knees to put pressure on the balls of your feet so you start skating backward in your new direction—the direction in which your heels are pointing. As you pivot and apply pressure you will glide backward, and from there you can choose to stride if needed. You can maintain and preserve speed with this technique.

Method Two: The Pivot

Drew Doughty is gliding forward on an angle while his head follows an oncoming play. To get his body to move backward and face the oncoming play while maintaining his forward speed, Doughty will need to reduce the weight on his blades (straighten his legs), pivot his heels toward his desired direction of travel and then thrust with the balls of his feet while gliding on his heels (backward stride).

Backward-to-Forward Transition

The backward-to-forward transition is an invaluable skill. There are numerous situations in which a seamless transition from skating backward to skating forward while staying square to your original direction of travel is needed, like when defending a rush and then having to advance for a turnover or when handling the puck backward and then advancing to make a play. The key is to maintain your momentum by not stopping in the transition.

Method

While striding backward, start making the transition to moving forward by centering your skates together, underneath you. Bend your knees and glide backward on both skates. Turn the toe of one of your skates out 90 degrees to the direction you are traveling in; this skate will become the drive skate for the first stride of your transition to the opposite direction. Plant your skate and put pressure on the inside edge of your blade by bending your knee and leaning forward, which will allow you to angle the blade and optimize your use of its inside edge. When you thrust, rock from being on a fully flat blade to being on the ball of your foot. This movement is very similar to a forward power start (see page 49).

Notes

It is important to maintain speed throughout your transition and to complete the transition without stopping. In order to do this, make sure that you are gliding backward on a flat blade. As well, your heels should touch when you bring your skates together as you begin the forward power start. This will stop you from stepping out of the transition, and it will help you perform a complete stride and begin the forward motion with a full extension. On the power start, the forward lean is essential to maintaining speed and even accelerating. As well, keeping the blade of the stick between your shoulders throughout this skating maneuver will help you maintain a proper body position.

Marc Staal

① Leaning forward helps Staal make a quick transition by allowing the maximum use of the inside edges on both skates, it also naturally leads the power from the transition in the right direction. Stick blade is kept on the ice between shoulders.

② Pressure is focused at the ball of the foot with the entire length of blade on the ice. Stall will thrust from the ball of his foot to begin quickly striding.

③ Foot is turned out and kept close to the ice for efficient, quick striding and recovery. The transition is a moving power start forward. Practice tapping your heels together underneath your body before your first stride to ensure a complete stride.

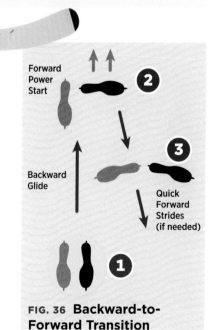

Forward Power Start

Backward Glide

Quick Forward Strides (if needed)

FIG. 36 Backward-to-Forward Transition

Back-Up and Turn

This is a backward-to-forward transition (or pivot) that allows you to go from skating backward to skating forward in the same direction.

Cross-Over Technique

Use this technique if you are skating backward and need to turn and skate forward with speed, like when chasing a player or a puck that is behind you.

While striding backward, reach one of your feet laterally to the side you wish to turn toward. Grab the ice with this skate, and, as you would in a cross-under (see page 43), draw the ice toward your body (this is like a reach and pull). As you draw the ice toward your glide skate, pivot your glide skate 90 degrees to the direction you wish to turn and rotate your upper body so you begin facing this same direction. Draw your skate underneath your body toward your glide skate and execute a cross-under behind and underneath your glide skate. Simultaneously, cross your glide skate over your cross-under skate (this is similar to power start forward with a cross-over; see page 49). As your cross-over skate lands, begin to stride forward in your desired direction as you recover your cross-under skate for the next stride.

Skate-to-Skate Technique

The second technique is a skate-to-skate turn, which is used to close the gap on a player who has moved laterally and is threatening to go past you.

While striding backward, reach one of your feet laterally to the side you wish to turn toward (toward the attacking player), grab the ice with this outstretched skate and draw the ice toward your body. Instead of crossing your drawing skate underneath your glide skate, pivot your glide skate 90 degrees to the direction you wish to turn, and tap your two skates together (very similar to the backward-to-forward transition). At the same time, begin to rotate your upper body so that you are facing into the turn. Stride forward beginning with your glide skate.

With the skate-to-skate technique, keep your skates near the ice at all times so you can adjust quickly to an attack move. The cross-over technique is often not suitable for closing the gap on an attacking player, as you will be unable to adjust to an attack move with your cross-over skate in the air. With both techniques be sure to quickly move your stick between your shoulders to lead you during the transition.

Forward-to-Forward Transition

There are times during a hockey game when you will be traveling forward in one direction and will almost immediately want to go forward in the opposite direction—all while not taking your eyes off the play (or puck). If you didn't have to watch the play, you could skate forward one way, execute a tight turn and very quickly start skating forward in the other direction. But when you want to keep your eye on the puck and maintain your speed, like when a puck-side winger moves back into a break-out position in the defensive zone, you need to execute a forward-to-forward transition.

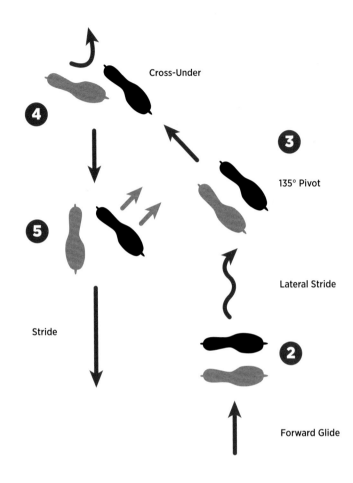

FIG. 37 Forward-to-Forward Transition

This is a very complicated move, mainly because while you are making the transition from forward in one direction to forward in the opposite direction you have to skate backward for a short period of time. The transition is broken into four parts, and it all starts with a lateral slide.

Slide

The key to maintaining your speed throughout this transition is to use a lateral slide (see page 47) into the transition instead of stopping. As you are skating forward, perform the lateral slide so that you are facing your desired direction (toward the play). The slide can be straight legged initially to reduce the amount of drag on your blades and increase your speed, but as you move into the transition you will have to bend your knees in order to accelerate.

Pivot

From your slide, pivot your heels so that you can glide backward. *Do not pivot 180 degrees* (which would send you backward on the same line you were already traveling in).

Instead, pivot 135 degrees (a little less than a half-turn) so that you are traveling backward in the same general direction but on a slight angle, away from the play. Keep your skates parallel, and glide with both skates on a flat blade.

Cross-Under

Once you are traveling backward, make your transition to go forward in the opposite direction by doing a cross-under (see page 43) followed by a stride forward. Perform the cross-under by using the back skate of your lateral slide to draw the ice toward and underneath the front skate of your lateral slide. The back skate is the cross-under skate. Remember to keep your knees bent. Rotate the cross-under skate as it passes beneath you and behind your other skate (which is gliding) so you can thrust with the outside edge of the blade at the pad of your foot. Add an ankle extension as you thrust to increase your speed.

Stride

As the cross-under skate recovers, stride forward, starting the first stride with your original front foot. Continue to stride forward with both feet to successfully complete a forward-to-forward transition.

Notes

The angle of the path you take when pivoting to skate backward will depend on how tight you intend the transition to be, how quickly you need to transition and how much room you have available. The less space and the quicker the desired transition, the sharper the backward angle should be. If you have a lot of space and time, the angle can be more open. Also, always keep the blade of your stick centered between your shoulders when executing the forward-to-forward transition. This will help you maintain a proper body position, balance and glide.

Cross-Under to Forward Stride

Jordan Staal is completing a forward-to-forward transition by crossing under as he sets off in his new direction. By keeping his stick blade centered between his shoulders, Staal is in proper position and ready to take a pass. As a centerman, Staal has many opportunities to use the forward-to-forward transition, given that he needs to backcheck deep into his defensive zone and then transition up the ice offensively to help lead the rush out of his end.

Latoral Skating

This technique will allow you to move laterally with speed and stability. It is used frequently, both when players are carrying the puck and when they are moving into open areas to create options for teammates. Defense often use this technique to change the point of attack when moving the puck across the blue line in the offensive zone. In the defensive or neutral zones, lateral skating can create a passing lane or space when you are being forechecked.

Brian Rafalski
Moving to the Off Side

1 Glide skate is flat and heel is pointing in the direction of travel. Rafalski's right knee is bent to allow for vertical weight transfers over the glide skate to increase speed.

2 Drive skate is recovering from a cross-under. For Rafalski to move quickly to his off side, he'll need to make quick, short cross-under strokes that are recovered rapidly.

3 Shoulders are rotated 90 degrees to the direction of travel and hands hold the stick in the hockey-playing position, which sets Rafalski up for a shot or pass.

It is essential that you are in a position to handle the puck, shoot and pass the puck or receive a pass while moving laterally. In order to move with speed and stability, one of your skates (the glide skate) must always be on the ice while your other skate (the drive skate) draws the ice toward your glide skate. A deep knee bend is essential during this maneuver, as are vertical weight transfers, which will provide additional speed.

Moving Toward the Off Side

This is when left-handed players move to their right and right-handed players move to their left. The drive skate is the off skate (the right skate for a left-handed player and the left skate for a right-handed player). The glide skate is the same skate. To move laterally, point the heel of your glide skate in your desired direction of travel. Next, reach and pull with your drive skate the way you would to initiate a cross-under, drawing the ice toward your glide skate with the inside edge of the entire blade of your drive skate. Draw the ice repeatedly with quick strokes, and execute your cross-unders with a quick recovery with your drive skate. Your glide skate stays on the ice on a flat blade.

When traveling toward the off side, your body should be positioned almost as if you were moving backward, similar to the technique used to skate backward around a curve.

Moving Toward the Proper Side

This is when left-handed players move to their left and right-handed players move to their right. Now the glide skate is the off skate (the right skate for a left-handed player and the left skate for a right-handed player). The drive skate is the same skate. The technique to move laterally to the proper side

is the same as to move laterally to the off side. Keep in mind, however, that when moving to the proper side, your upper body has to be rotated to remain square so you can shoot or pass the puck at any time. Your upper body should be opened up to be 90 degrees to your direction of travel. This is a very challenging skill to master. Players who can acquire this skill can pick up pucks on their off side at the boards along the blue line in the offensive zone (on their backhand), and they can then move laterally across the blue line toward the middle of the rink for a shot or a pass.

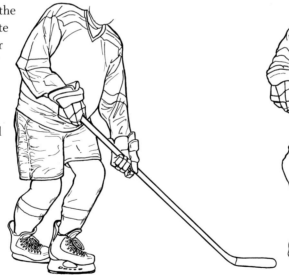

FIG. 38 Moving to Off Side
Player shoots left and is moving laterally to the right — the off side. Position of shoulders, arms, torso and hips is very similar to skating backward. The right skate (off-side skate) drives, and the left skate (same-side skate) stays on the ice and glides.

FIG. 39
Moving to Proper Side
Player shoots left and is moving laterally to the left — the proper side. Shoulders, arms and torso need to be rotated to the left to keep the puck in a position where it can be passed or shot. The right skate (off-side skate) stays on the ice and glides, and the left skate (same-side skate) drives.

Tight Turns

A tight turn is a great tool to use to create space or close a gap. Offensively, you can use a tight turn to evade players, maintain puck possession or release from a checker to get open. Defensively, the ability to turn tightly will allow you to maintain a good defensive position and take away the space of your opponent.

Ryan Smyth
Tight Turn to the Backhand

1 Stick blade enters the turn first, followed by the inside skate and the outside skate. Blade is cupped to control the puck on the backhand.

2 Top hand is held up and away from the body to keep the puck close to the lead skate. The higher and further away Smyth moves his top hand, and the further down the shaft he slides his bottom hand, the closer the puck will be to his lead foot.

3 Pressure applied by the outside edge of the lead skate slows Smyth down so that he can execute the turn at a manageable speed. When Smyth goes to exit the turn he will thrust off the heel of his back skate to propel him in his new direction.

Entering the Turn

When you enter a tight turn, you need to be in the hockey-playing position. Extend the skate that will be on the inside of the turn forward with a flat blade and lean your body in that direction, keeping your knee over the extended foot with a forward body lean. You should be using the outside edge of your inside skate and the inside edge of your outside skate. Enter the turn with your stick blade first, then with your inside knee/skate and then with your outside skate. You can determine the path of your turn by the way you position your lead skate. The tighter the turn, the closer your lead skate should be to your body and the more you need to bend your lead leg. The more gradual the turn, the further your lead skate should be from your body. To generate more speed on the turn, thrust with a heel push from your back foot. Keeping your feet on the same trajectory also enhances speed.

Through the Turn

Keep your top hand away from your body on the backhand and across your body and underneath the forearm of your bottom arm on the forehand. This promotes glide and puck control (see page 78). Rotate the top hand to cup the puck. Drive the inside knee forward and use a heel push from your outside skate to maintain speed, or even accelerate, through the turn.

Exiting the Turn

As you come to the end of your turn, increase your speed by driving your inside knee forward, moving it further over and in front of your lead skate. This will keep your body low to the ice, help protect the puck and, most importantly, maximize your glide. To come out of the tight turn with

FIG. 40 Tight Turn to the Forehand
Top hand is brought across the body and underneath the forearm of the bottom hand to allow the stick blade to cup the puck and lead the turn, keeping the blade close to the lead foot. Knee is thrust ahead of the lead skate to protect the puck and to increase the weight over the lead skate, adding glide to the turn.

FIG. 41 Tight Turn to the Backhand
Top hand is held up and away from the body and bottom hand is stretched across the body to keep the stick close to the lead foot. Knee is thrust over the lead skate to protect the puck and to increase the weight over and in front of the lead skate, adding glide to the turn.

speed, use a heel push off your back skate. Then, thrust off the inside edge at the ball of your foot and cross this skate over your lead skate. As your back skate crosses over, cross-under with your lead skate. An elite player like Sidney Crosby can reach forward with his lead skate and draw the ice toward himself before he executes a strong cross-under (and ankle extension) with his lead skate—which catapults him into a drive out of the tight turn. After your tight turn, try moving forward laterally with a few quick cross-over/under combos.

Slowing Down

If you are going too fast when you are entering a turn and need to slow yourself down in order to execute the turn effectively, rotate your lead skate and thrust it laterally in your direction of travel (with your toes facing into the turn and your heel facing away from turn). The inside arch of your foot should be facing away from you so you can use the outside edge of your skate (the edge closest to your body) to scrape the ice with a flat, lateral blade. Elite skaters use this technique to enter into a tight turn at a very high speed and control their speed through the turn.

Drive and Delay

In some quarters this technique is called the Bobby Orr escape move, as No. 4 made the drive and delay a part of his regular on-ice repertoire. In a drive and delay, you accelerate on a curve in one direction—drive—and then quickly turn in a tight glide away from the path of the original turn—delay. This technique creates space and is used in many situations: driving the net with the puck only to be cut off by a defensive player then delaying to create space and options, driving over the blue line into the offensive zone and then delaying toward the boards, or avoiding forecheckers in your own zone by driving toward your own net and then delaying into the corner.

Drive

The driving part of this technique is simple. Accelerate by using the forward cross-over technique (see page 38) to make a strong drive on a curve.

Delay

When you have reached the point when you want to delay, you need to go from crossing over to a tight turn. To do this, you need to drive off the inside edge of your cross-over skate (your outside skate) the same as you would for a cross-over, but before your skate crosses over and contacts the ice, you need to rotate your foot away from your initial direction of travel so that your foot will be facing your new direction of travel. The inside arch of your foot should be facing away from you, and when you plant your foot on the ice, your skate should be angled so that you are using your outside edge (also known as an outside-edge reverse). This skate will become your lead skate for the tight turn.

Once you are on the outside edge of your lead skate, bring your other foot (your inside skate on the cross-over) around to follow your lead foot. This foot will now become your outside skate in the tight turn, and it will be your drive skate. As in a tight turn, you will drive off the inside edge of the heel of the outside skate to maintain speed or even accelerate through the turn.

Notes

When you initiate the delay, ensure that you are in a deep knee bend, with the knee of your lead leg driving forward. This gives you the proper positioning to maximize glide on the tight turn and to create space. It is critical that you position your hands properly through the cross-overs and then quickly change their position when moving into the delay (see page 80). This will help you maintain speed and even accelerate. It will also help you control and protect the puck.

Steven Stamkos

1 Right foot is turned away from the initial direction of travel (driving to the forehand) and pressure is applied to the outside edge of the blade (outside-edge reverse) in order to pursue the new direction of travel (delay to the backhand). Back foot will follow the right foot as the stick blade leads toward the new direction in a tight turn to the backhand.

2 Top and bottom arm have moved from a forehand drive position and are pushed out from the body with rotated wrists in order to cradle the puck on the backhand. This movement must be made quickly.

3 Knees are bent, especially the back knee, and Stamkos will use a vertical weight transfer coupled with a heel push to accelerate through the tight turn.

Heel-to-Heel Turn

Skating heel to heel allows you to open up and face into a turn while handling the puck. It is very effective when executing wraparounds, as it allows you to open up, accelerate using the thrust of the trailing skate and see the position of the goalie and defenders. It also makes you a constant threat through the turn, as you are always in a position to pass or shoot the puck, even though you are turning. Sidney Crosby uses the heel-to-heel turn frequently to maintain puck possession while creating scoring chances.

Dan Boyle

1 Forward body lean keeps Boyle on the inside edge of both his skates.

2 Hands are in the hockey-playing position, meaning Boyle is a threat to shoot or pass.

3 Thrust is from the inside edge of the left (trailing) skate at the ball of the foot, sending Boyle on a curve to his right (forehand). The heel of his drive skate glides, as does his entire right (lead) skate. Knees are bent to provide vertical weight transfers.

Method

To execute a heel-to-heel turn, you need to open your hips and rotate both of your skates so your toes face out and your heels are together. Your lead skate should point toward your direction of travel, and your trailing skate should point toward the direction you came from. The gap between your skates can be from a hand width to shoulder width apart, with the wider stance being more stable. To ensure proper glide, and even acceleration, you need to use a deep knee bend with vertical weight transfers, as well as thrusts from the inside edges of both skates (from the ball of the trailing foot and the heel of the lead foot). Make sure the angle of your skates allows you to use your inside edges. The main thrust on the turn should come from the ball of your trailing skate. Your glide is generated on the heel of your trailing skate and on the entire blade of your front skate.

Notes

Turning heel to heel is generally more gradual than a tight turn. Some players will alternate between a tight turn and a heel-to-heel turn when carrying the puck. A tight turn will put you in a better position to protect the puck if there is pressure, while the heel-to-heel turn puts you in a better position to open up and see more of the ice to make a play. Generally, players use the heel-to-heel turn to move to their forehand. Advanced players add vertical weight transfers to the turn to increase the thrust they are generating by "rocking" their skates—bending their knees and moving their ankles up and down to put added pressure on the ball of the trailing foot and the heel of the lead foot. This can be particularly effective when using the heel-to-heel turn for a wraparound.

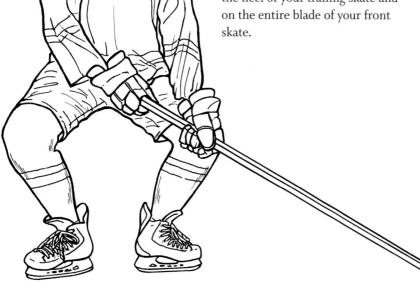

FIG. 42 Deep Bend

With your knees deeply bent you get more pressure on your edges, which can be turned into speed and power when you use vertical weight transfers and thrusts from the ball of your lead foot and the heel of your trailing foot. A deep knee bend also allows your hands to be closer to the ice, enabling you to push the puck further away from you as you slide your bottom hand toward your top hand. The extended reach coupled with the powerful drive makes this an excellent option for a wraparound from behind the net.

4 Puckhandling

Sidney Crosby performs a a tight turn to the backhand. See page 78 for more on handling a puck through a tight turn.

Holding the Stick

When moving forward or backward in a straight line while puckhandling, you need to keep your blade, arms and hands in a position that allows you to quickly and effectively execute a pass, shot or a deke.

Evgeni Malkin

1 Top of the stick is held with the correct top-hand grip (see page 22), which allows proper wrist rolling for effective puckhandling. Top hand is kept out and away from the body keeping the top-hand elbow down and the stick blade square to the ice.

2 Bottom hand is in the middle of the body, not to the side, for efficient puck control and protection; it also grips the stick loosely in order to slide up or down the shaft for a puckhandling maneuver, a pass or a shot.

3 Stick blade is square to the ice and in the middle of the body, which allows a move to the forehand or backhand. Blade is closed slightly to cup the puck on the forehand. With the proper top-hand grip, the stick can be rotated while puckhandling so it can close over the puck on the backhand and the forehand.

FIG. 43 Properly held stick
Keep your arms out from your body and your stick blade square on the ice in the middle of your body. You will need to bend your knees and lean forward — key elements to your stance.

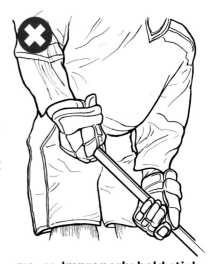

FIG. 44 Improperly held stick
You cannot have a proper stance if your top hand is stuck on your hip, as you will be further upright and your elbow will jut out past your back. You will not be able to properly handle or pass the puck.

Proper Arm Position

When puckhandling with two hands on your stick and skating forward, you should line up your hands with the middle of your body and hold them out in front of you. Your bottom hand will be in the center of your body and your top hand will be between the center of your body and your off-side hip. It is crucial that you extend your arms out from your body enough so that, if viewed from the side, the elbow of your top hand does not jut out past your back, becoming visible behind you. You should place your hands so that your stick blade is square on the ice. This ensures that your body and arms are in the proper position and that the puck is in the proper position in relation to your body to be effectively puckhandled. If your elbow protrudes past your back when you handle the puck, you are either handling the puck too close to your body or your stick is too long.

Similarly, your arms should be in the same position when you are handling a puck when moving backward as when you are handling it when moving forward. Keeping your top hand away from your body will make handling a puck when going backward much easier. A common puckhandling mistake is for players to not extend their top hand out from their body, which results in the top hand being "stuck" on the player's hip, severely limiting the player's ability to handle the puck.

Tension

Another common mistake made by players learning to puckhandle, or trying to learn more advanced puckhandling skills, is to grip the stick too tightly. Your bottom hand has to be loose so you can freely move the stick and so you can quickly move your hand up and down the stick. Similarly, the tension of your top hand has to be light, with the exception of your little finger and third finger, which should grip firmly. Your wrists and arms have to be relaxed to allow quick and flexible maneuvers.

Rolling Your Wrists

Rolling your wrists is *the* fundamental puckhandling movement. When rolling your wrists you create a cradling or cupping effect with the blade of your stick that allows you to control the puck. You must be able to roll your wrists in order to increase the control and range of movement that is available to you when handling the puck away from your body—it will also help you perform more advanced puckhandling skills. It is essential that you become adept at rolling your wrists with your hands and arms in various positions in order to master advanced puckhandling moves.

Jason Spezza

1 Stick is held with the proper top-hand grip, and wrist is rolled to cup the puck on the forehand.

2 Bottom hand is loosely holding the stick to allow the shaft to rotate and move up and down through the bottom hand as needed. Wrist is rolled to help Spezza handle the puck in close to the body and to cup the puck.

Practice

In order to cup the blade around or toward the puck, you must rotate your top hand by rolling your wrist. Here is the best way to learn how to roll your wrists:

1 While in the hockey-playing position with a puck in front of you and in the middle of your body and with both hands on your stick, place the heel of your stick on the puck.

2 Rotate your top hand so the toe of the stick touches the ice on one side and then on the other side of the puck. On your first attempt keep your bottom-hand grip loose so you can feel the shaft of the stick turn in your palm. On your second pass, grip with your bottom hand more tightly so that it too is rotating with the top hand. Repetition of this rotation is called rolling your wrists.

3 Try rotating with your top hand only and then with your bottom hand only. Use a proper grip and rotate your hands so that the palm of each hand is facing up and then down.

Method

To puckhandle, stand in the hockey-playing position with a puck in front of you and in the middle of your body and roll your wrists. Start with the stick on the ice beside the puck and lift the stick ever so slightly over the puck as you alternately cup the puck with the front of the blade and then cup the puck with the back of the blade. When you are not lifting the stick over the puck, there should be as much contact as possible between the blade and the puck. Handle the puck in the middle of the blade. As you progress, practice handling the puck toward the heel and the toe of the blade, always keeping the blade square to the ice.

FIG. 45 Backhand
Proper hand and wrist position to cup the puck on the backhand while in the hockey-playing position.

FIG. 46 Forehand
Proper hand and wrist position to cup the puck on the forehand while in the hockey-playing position.

FIG. 47 Blade Rotation
Proper blade rotation for cupping the puck on the backhand and forehand while executing basic puckhandling.

Extending Your Reach

Players can greatly benefit from being able to move the puck away from their body, either to their forehand side or to their backhand side. This move can be used to deke a player, to change the angle or point of attack before a shot or a pass, or simply to avoid a stick check and keep possession of the puck.

FIG. 48 Backhand Extension
Move your top hand out and away from your body on your backhand side. Slide your bottom hand up, toward your top hand. Roll your wrists to cup the puck, and extend further by bending your off-side knee. To increase your extension, cross your same-side skate over your off-side skate.

FIG. 49 Forehand Extension
Bring your top hand underneath the forearm of your bottom hand and slide your bottom hand up, toward your top hand. Roll your wrists to cup the puck, and extend further by bending your same-side knee. To increase your extension, cross your off-side skate over your same-side skate.

Jason Blake

1 Top of the stick is held with the correct top-hand grip (see page 22), which allows the blade to be rolled closed on the backhand to keep control of the puck. Blake can further extend his reach by straightening his top-hand elbow and by sliding his bottom hand further up the shaft to meet his top hand.

2 Bottom hand is high on the shaft, toward the top hand, to help maximize the two-handed extension; grip is loose unless shooting or passing.

3 Stick blade is rotated to cup the puck on the backhand.

Forehand Extension

To extend the puck away from your body to your forehand side, stand in the hockey-playing position and move the puck to your forehand. Extend your reach by bringing your top hand across your body to your forehand side. Move your bottom hand up the shaft of the stick as you extend the blade away from your body and cup the puck. As you extend your reach, push your top hand under the forearm of your bottom hand so that the blade is square to the ice and the toe is pointed ahead. For most players, when they are at maximum extension their bottom hand will be close to one fist-length from their top hand. This will allow you to pass or shoot when your reach is extended to your forehand side. Some elite players are able to extend their reach to the point that their bottom hand will touch their top hand.

Backhand Extension

To extend the puck out to your backhand side, push your top arm away from your body on your backhand side and move your bottom hand across your body and up the shaft of the stick. The closer your bottom hand is to your top hand, the further away the blade will be from your body. At maximum extension your bottom hand will be touching your top hand. Elite players can handle the puck and pass or shoot the puck from this position.

Forehand Extension

Ryan Getzlaf drives past Travis Moen with the puck extended to his forehand to keep the puck from being knocked off his stick. Getzlaf's top hand is under the forearm of his bottom hand and his stick blade is square to the ice. Note Getzlaf's glide on a flat blade and his deep knee bend.

Extra Extension

The further you extend your reach, to either your backhand side or your forehand side, the straighter your arms need to be and the more your hands will be pushed away from your body. To increase your extension you can "break" your wrists, which is extreme wrist rolling. You break your wrists so that the blade angles away from you as far as it can. To further increase your extension, you can lower your hands and bend the knee closest to the puck. Putting your hands and body closer to the ice enables you to extend further then you would be able to from an upright position, and it gives you better puck control and puck protection. Extra extension will help you avoid defenders getting "stick on puck."

One-Handed Extensions

One-handed extensions to the forehand and backhand are great moves to use when driving around a defender, as you can use the hand that was removed from the stick to help protect the puck from defenders pressuring from the inside.

To extend your reach to your backhand side with one hand, remove your bottom hand from the stick and extend the blade away from your body by pushing your top hand out, rolling your hand palm-down to cup the puck.

To extend your reach to your forehand side with one hand, remove your top hand from the stick and extend the blade away from your body by pushing your bottom hand out while rolling your hand palm-down to cup the puck.

One-Handed Extension to Reach for a Puck

Anze Kopitar maximizes his reach to get to a loose puck. His top arm and hand are raised to increase his reach and keep his stick blade square to the ice. Kopitar maximizes this effort by keeping his front foot underneath his body for balance and support as he bends his knee that's closest to the puck while extending his other leg out, allowing him to lean forward — so far that his chest is almost touching his knee. Kopitar could not be any lower to the ice while still skating.

Tight Turns, Delays, Transitions and Lateral Handling

When executing these four distinct skating moves with the puck—tight turns, drive and delay, forward-to-backward transitions and lateral skating—your ability to handle the puck with control and with speed is affected greatly by the position of your hands. Speed with the puck will allow you to use these maneuvers to create space and make plays.

Tight-Turn Puckhandling

When turning tightly to your forehand side, bring your top hand across your body to your forehand side and position it underneath the forearm of your bottom arm so that your top and bottom arms are crossed. Roll both of your wrists to cup the puck.

When turning tightly to your backhand side, push your top hand away from your body, extend your arms and roll both of your wrists to cup the puck.

In both instances, keep your knees bent (a deep knee bend with your lead knee will promote glide and help protect the puck) and your hands elevated in order to keep the blade of your stick square on the ice.

Drive and Delay

The drive and delay is a combination of a forward cross-over—the drive—with a tight turn to create space—the delay. Players can use it anywhere on the ice to separate from a defender and create space to make a play.

When doing a drive with the puck, start with your arms and hands in the same position they are in when doing forward cross-overs, with your hands rotated to cup the puck (see page 38). Then, during the delay, move your top and bottom hands quickly across your body to the position used in a tight turn. Remember, you are changing direction and so is the puck, so you'll need to roll your wrists to reverse the rotation of your stick blade in order to cup the puck with the other side of the blade.

If you were driving to your proper side with forward cross-overs you would delay away from the play with a tight turn to your backhand side. If you were driving to your off side with forward cross-overs you would delay away from the play with a tight turn to your forehand side.

Forward-to-Backward Transition

When skating forward with the puck and reversing your direction to travel backward the way you came (see page 53), the transition between forward and backward presents a puckhandling challenge not unlike the drive and delay: to evade your opponent you need to keep control of the puck as you quickly change direction.

If you are skating forward and you initiate the forward-to-backward transition with your rear

Advanced Forehand Tight Turn

When you turn tightly to your forehand it is very difficult to shoot or pass the puck quickly, as you are not in a shooting position. This is a disadvantage if you are turning into a scoring situation. Elite players can do a tight turn to the forehand and be in a shooting or passing position by lowering their top hand and moving it and their bottom hand away from and across their body toward their backhand side, keeping the blade of their stick square to their direction of travel. Their wrists are rolled to control the puck, and their hands are away from their body so they can quickly shoot or pass.

Evgeni Malkin
Forehand Tight Turn

1 Top hand is brought across the body and underneath the forearm of the bottom hand in order to handle the puck along the trajectory of the turn while keeping the puck in front of the body and in between the shoulders. Malkin's top hand is held up against his arm and away from his waist and hip in order to keep his stick blade flat on the ice.

2 Bottom-hand grip is firm and arm is extended as the top hand comes across. Both wrists are rolled to cup the puck on the forehand. Markin's hands may change position throughout the turn to keep the stick blade square on the ice and the same distance from his body.

Drive and Delay with a Backhand Tight Turn

After driving to the forehand, Sidney Crosby is delaying with a tight turn to the backhand. In order to handle the puck along the trajectory of the turn, Crosby needs to push his top hand away from his body and rotate it to cup the puck. Crosby is using a heel push from his back skate for thrust, an outside-edge lateral slide on his front skate to maintain control and a deep knee bend of his lead leg for glide and to help protect the puck.

toward your off side (backhand side), you should push your top hand away from your body and rotate your hands to cup the puck with the back of the blade (like a tight turn to your backhand side). Keeping your hands in this position throughout the transition will help you handle the puck at a high speed.

When you initiate the forward-to-backward transition with your rear toward your same side

(forehand side), push your top hand across your body and under the forearm of your bottom hand and rotate your hands to cup the puck with the front of the blade (like a tight turn to your forehand side). Again, keep your hands in this position throughout the transition. Once you begin striding straight backward you will begin to puckhandle as you typically do when skating backward.

Lateral Handling: Toward the Off or Proper Side

Defense often move toward the off or proper side in the offensive zone when they have the puck and are moving along the blue line. This skill enables them to move toward the middle of the ice for a shot or pass.

Method

When moving laterally toward the off side (backhand side) with the puck, carry the puck in a manner similar to when you execute a tight turn to your forehand side: push your top hand across your body toward your forehand side and keep your hands rotated to cup the puck on the front of the blade. However, you do not have to bring your top hand far across your body and under the forearm of your bottom hand the way you do when making a tight turn as you will generally be moving in a straighter line. The more curved the direction in which you are moving, the more you should extend your top hand under your bottom arm for control. The straighter your direction, the less your top hand needs to come across your body.

When you are moving laterally toward your proper side (forehand side) with the puck, initially you should position your hands and arms similarly to when you are doing a tight turn to your backhand side: push your top hand away from your body and rotate your hands so the puck is cupped on the back of the blade. As you continue to move laterally, move the puck toward and then onto your forehand side and try to remain square with your target by rotating your upper body. This will enable you to shoot or pass, but it is a very challenging skill.

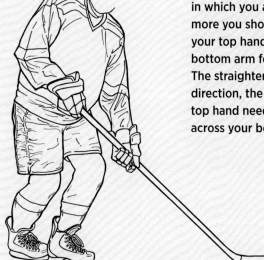

FIG. 50 Handling to the Off Side
The hand position shown is for when you are moving laterally in a straight line toward your off side. The more curved your path, the more your top hand needs to move across your body toward (and possibly underneath) your bottom forearm, as you would for a tight turn on your forehand (see page 63). When moving laterally to your off side, you will shoot or pass off your off foot.

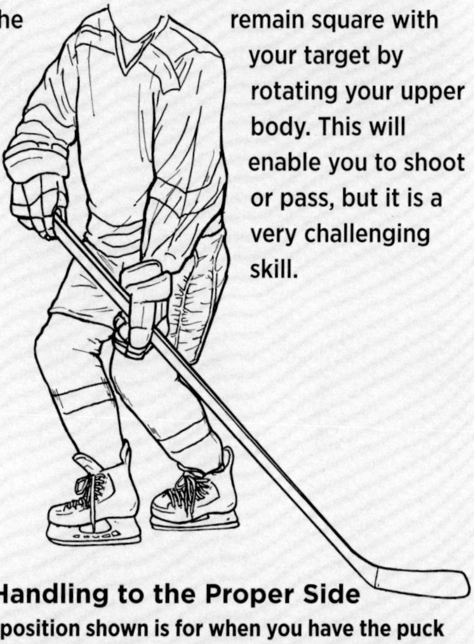

FIG. 51 Handling to the Proper Side
The hand position shown is for when you have the puck on the forehand side of your blade and are ready to pass or shoot. However, when moving to your proper side you will more than likely start with the puck on the back of your blade, closer to your off side. This will look similar to a tight turn to your backhand (see page 63), with your top hand away from your body and rotated to carry the puck on the back of your blade. To move the puck from your backhand to your forehand, continue to move laterally and move the puck across your body to your forehand side. Rotate your shoulders and torso to remain square to your target (as pictured).

5 Passing

Henrik Sedin makes a same-foot pass.
See page 84 for more on passing.

Making a Pass: Forehand or Backhand

Hockey is a team game. It is also a game of puck possession. In order to keep possession of the puck, players need to be able to pass it accurately. The very best players are great passers and pass receivers who are able to make all the players around them better.

Michael Del Zotto
Long Forehand Pass

1 Head is up and looking at target. The puck, which started "back of center," has been swept forward to the release point. As the puck moves across the body, the top hand moves across the chest and is kept away from the body while the bottom hand moves toward the center of the body and the shoulder of that arm drops.

2 Hips and legs continue to point 90 degrees to the target. The hips and legs will flex under the torque of the passing motion, but only the shoulders and torso fully rotate.

3 Del Zotto will finish his long pass by rolling his wrists over and pointing the toe of his stick at the target.

Method

Stand in the hockey-skating position with your skates 90 degrees to your target. Roll your wrists to put the puck in the middle of the blade, keep your head up and look at your target. You should be in the same position you are in when puckhandling while moving forward, with your top hand out from your body. To initiate the passing motion, bring the puck back of "center" (an imaginary line drawn on the ice running up between your skates)—this motion will bring your top hand across your body to your same side during a forehand pass and across your body to your off side during a backhand pass. From this position, with the puck cradled and back of center, sweep the puck toward your target with the blade of your stick square to the target. Release the puck from the center of the blade and follow through with your stick. For a long pass, roll your wrists over and follow through by pointing the blade of your stick at your target; for a short pass, follow through by moving both your top and bottom hands away from your body, keeping the blade square to your target. In both forehand and backhand passes, the top hand travels across your body.

Backhand Pass

Mike Ribeiro looks to make a backhand pass. The puck is back of center, and Ribeiro's stick is rotated to cup the puck and sweep it forward. Like in a forehand pass, his shoulders and torso rotate while his feet stay 90 degrees to his target. Most importantly, Ribeiro's top hand stays out from his body for strength and accuracy.

FIG. 52 Short Pass

When passing to a teammate close to you, use a short follow-through: move both your top and bottom hands away from your body and keep your blade square to your target.

Tip

Practice making passes when stationary and with your feet 90 degrees to your target (duplicating two players skating forward in the same direction) as well as with your feet facing your target. Practice making passes both off two feet and off one foot and, in particular, off your same foot (i.e. left foot for left-handed players and right foot for right-handed players). Practice these passes while in motion, too.

You can also work on quick-release passes—receiving and making a pass in one motion. Remember to always try to sweep the puck. Even with quick-release passes, the pass should be received by rolling your wrists and cupping the puck, and then it should be quickly swept toward the target, not snapped. It is also important to keep your top hand away from your body to ensure your passes are controlled and accurate. This is particularly true with backhand passes, as many players tend to have their top hand too close to their body on a backhand pass, resulting in weak and inaccurate passes. The sweeping motion and follow-through of a backhand pass will take your top hand across your body.

Same-Foot Pass
Patrick Kane makes a short distance same-foot pass. Instead of a traditional pass that sweeps the puck from back foot to front foot, Kane faces his target head-on and sweeps the puck from behind his right heel on his forehand side to ahead of his same foot on his forehand side. Kane extends his arms away from his body while placing his weight over his same foot. Upon release, his stick blade will rise up and stay square to his target, like in Fig 52.

Receiving a Pass

The key to controlling your reception of a pass is to reverse the motion you make when releasing a pass.

Method

Receiving a puck to your stick is a lot like catching a football: you must absorb the energy from the object. In order to do this, move your stick away from your body and extend your arms slightly toward your target as you bring the blade out to "meet" the puck (especially for pucks that are passed with a lot of force). It is crucial that you keep your stick on the ice with the blade square to the ice, which provides a target for the passer. Upon receiving the puck, "catch" the pass by rolling your wrists so that the blade moves back and cups the puck. This absorbs the energy of the pass and helps you control the puck. Keeping your top hand away from your body and rotating your top hand to cup the blade are keys to successfully receiving passes on your backhand.

FIG. 53 Backhand Reception
The principals used to receive a pass on the forehand apply to the backhand. This is how your blade should be cupped when catching the pass, as it will help you control the puck by absorbing the energy of the pass.

Sam Gagner

1 Hands are kept out from body as Gagner brings his stick out to meet the pass.

2 Stick blade is being brought to the ice in anticipation of the pass. Upon reception of the pass, Gagner will rotate his top hand to cup his blade to "catch" the pass, and his arms and the blade of his stick will move in toward his body to help absorb the energy of the pass.

Receiving Off-Target Passes

The key to controlling your reception of an off-target pass is to keep your stick blade square to the ice, as opposed to having only the heel or the toe of the blade receive the pass.

Receiving Off-Target Passes on the Forehand

To receive a pass anywhere between the heel of your stick and your off skate, or even outside your off skate, move your stick blade to the puck by keeping your top hand up and away from your body. Slide your bottom hand low on the shaft of your stick while you lower your body. This ensures your blade is flat and square to the puck. The closer the puck is to your off foot, the further your bottom hand must move down the shaft of your stick and the further your top hand will be pushed to your off side.

Elite players will lower their body, sometimes to the point of putting a knee on the ice, to shoot the puck after receiving the pass. This technique has been used effectively by players like Sidney Crosby and Mario Lemieux to shoot pucks off of passes that are well in on their feet.

If the pass is coming so quickly at your feet that you don't have time to get the stick blade into position, use your skate blade to receive the pass and deflect the puck to your stick or to where you can reach the puck and bring it under control. Angle your skate blade to deflect the puck to where you want it to go.

When the pass is ahead of the blade, accept the pass by extending

Thomas Vanek
Receiving in Feet

1 Shoulders are square to the incoming puck and head is up. Vanek's top-hand and arm are raised and pushed out from his body so he can place the stick blade between his feet, which are spread wide.

2 Bottom hand is low on the shaft of the stick to keep the blade square to the ice. Vanek's right elbow is pinched in by his chest, and his bottom hand is thrust forward, away from his body, the same distance as his top hand.

3 Stick blade is being brought to the ice in anticipation of the pass. Vanek will further bend his knees, move his hands out toward the puck and then move his hands downward in order to get his blade square to the ice.

and moving the stick blade forward, keeping it square to the puck. To do this, extend your top hand away from your body and move your bottom hand progressively up the shaft until, at the furthest point, it touches your top hand. To reach even further, release your bottom hand from the stick, extending and allowing your top hand to move the stick further ahead so the blade can receive the pass.

Receiving Off-Target Passes on the Backhand

If you are receiving an off-target pass on your off side on the backhand side of your blade, whether in your feet or ahead of you, you use the same hand movements as when receiving an off-target pass on your forehand. If the pass is between the heel of your stick and your off skate, move your bottom hand down the shaft of your stick and move your top hand across

Receiving an Off-Target Pass Toward Your Same Side on the Backhand
Paul Kariya moves his top hand across his body and under the forearm of his bottom hand to receive a pass in his feet toward his same side, using the backhand side of his stick blade. Kariya's hand position ensures his blade will stay square to the ice.

FIG. 54

Passes Ahead of You
Keep both feet planted on the ice and extend your reach by moving your top hand as far across your body as you can. At the same time bring your bottom hand up toward your top hand. Keep your arm raised to keep your blade square to the ice.

your body and out from your body toward your offside.

If the pass is ahead of your stick blade, extend your reach by raising your top hand toward the puck and bring your bottom hand progressively up the shaft of your stick toward your top hand. This is will keep your blade square to the ice as you extend your reach.

If you are receiving the pass between the heel of your stick and your feet on the backhand side of your blade toward your same side, bring your top hand across your body toward the forearm of your bottom hand. The closer the puck is to your feet, the further your top hand will move across your body and underneath the forearm of your bottom hand.

Saucer Pass

Sometimes you will need to pass the puck over an opposing player's stick or even their leg or body. In this instance you will want the puck to go up off the ice, over the obstacle and then return to the ice flat so the receiving player can handle the pass. The best way to do this is to use a saucer pass. This type of pass gets its name from the fact that the puck travels in the air like a saucer or Frisbee. It stays flat while it rotates through the air and when it lands on the ice.

Andrew Brunette
Snap Saucer Pass

1 Brunette's hands are moving from his left to his right in order to make the puck travel from the heel of his stick to the toe of his stick as he snap passes the puck. Hands are kept away from his body so they are free to move quickly in order to release the puck and add rotation to the puck.

2 Pass has just left the toe of Brunette's stick. The velocity of his open blade quickly striking the puck at the stick's heel, coupled with his hand movement toward his right side while raising his stick off the ice during his follow-through, caused the puck to rapidly snap off the toe of the stick.

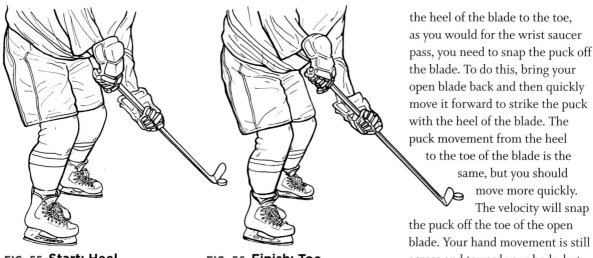

FIG. 55 Start: Heel
Start your wrist saucer pass with the puck slightly ahead of you on your stick side. Keep your hands away from your body and to your forehand side. The puck is at the heel of your stick. Keep your blade open and your knees bent.

FIG. 56 Finish: Toe
Quickly bring your hands in toward your body and move them across your body toward your off side. This will roll the puck, from the heel to the toe, along your open stick blade. As the puck reaches the toe, raise your stick off the ice as you follow through to your off side. If your blade is open and you move your hands very quickly, this will spin the puck and send it airborne.

Wrist Saucer

The "wrist" saucer pass is the easiest version of the saucer pass. Start by opening the blade of your stick (a closed blade is one that cups the puck) with the puck on the heel of the angled blade. Initiate the pass with both of your hands away from your body and with your shoulders square to your target. Quickly move your hands across your body toward your backhand side. This movement will simultaneously move your hands in toward your body as it sends the puck from the heel of the blade to the toe, where it is released—you are cutting your blade across the puck. The harder and quicker you do this (along with how open the blade is), the higher, faster and flatter your pass will be.

The puck will spin counterclockwise for a left-handed player and clockwise for a right-handed player as it travels through the air.

Snap Saucer

The closer the receiving player is to you, the more difficult it is for you to make a good saucer pass. For very short passes, a "snap" saucer pass is more efficient: it gets the puck in the air quickly with a quicker release. This technique is often used when the puck is in a passing position away from your body.

The technique for the snap saucer pass is the same as for the wrist saucer pass, except that instead of rolling the puck from the heel of the blade to the toe, as you would for the wrist saucer pass, you need to snap the puck off the blade. To do this, bring your open blade back and then quickly move it forward to strike the puck with the heel of the blade. The puck movement from the heel to the toe of the blade is the same, but you should move more quickly. The velocity will snap the puck off the toe of the open blade. Your hand movement is still across and toward your body, but your hands do not have to travel as far, allowing you to release the puck more quickly. It takes much more practice to be accurate with a snap saucer pass than with a wrist saucer pass. Many players use a snap saucer pass when executing a backhand saucer pass.

Tip

To practice spinning the puck, pass with a teammate using the technique outlined above but keep the puck on the ice. Try to see how quickly you can move your hands in order to make the puck spin as quickly as possible. Once you are able to spin the puck and slide it on the ice to your target, then you can start to grip the puck more with the heel of the blade and follow through higher with the blade after you release the puck in order to start to lift it off the ice while it rotates. Eventually you will be able to lift the puck right off the ice and perform a perfect saucer pass.

6 Shooting

Alex Ovechkin releases a slap shot.
See page 104 for more on slap shots.

Wrist Shot

This is the shot most players will learn first. It can be very accurate, especially if you keep your head up through the shooting motion.

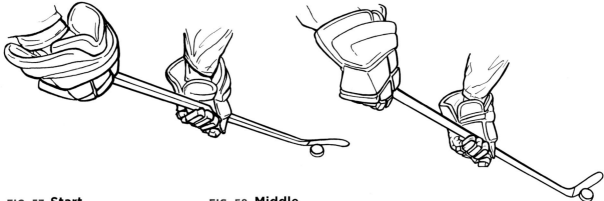

FIG. 57 Start

Begin a traditional wrist shot with the puck back of center and at the heel of your stick. Roll your wrists to keep your blade closed.

FIG. 58 Middle

Roll your wrists and open your blade as you sweep the puck toward your front foot. Move the puck along your open blade toward the middle of the blade. As you come closer to your front foot, quickly roll your wrists and close your blade as you release. The entire wrist-rolling movement, from start to release (breaking your wrists), must be done very quickly.

Technique

The technique of a traditional wrist shot is similar to the technique of a forehand pass. When executing a basic wrist shot, stand 90 degrees to your target with your skates parallel. Bring the puck back of center (an imaginary line drawn on the ice running up between your skates), and then sweep the puck forward while you transfer your weight from your back skate (the skate furthest from the target) to your front skate (the skate closest to the target).

All in the Wrists

With the puck back of center, roll your wrists to close your blade over the puck and "grip" the puck with the heel of the blade. As you sweep the puck forward, roll your wrists to open the blade up, allowing the puck to travel toward the middle of the blade. Upon release, roll your wrists a third time, closing the blade over the puck and whipping it off the middle of the blade toward the toe. The entire motion is: blade closed, open, closed.

Weight and Follow-Through

As you pull the puck back, move your hands back and in slightly toward your body, and keep your weight on your back foot with your back leg bent. Quickly sweep the puck forward as close to your body as comfortably possible, and quickly transfer your weight to your front skate, bending your front leg. Release the shot from the center of your body, and move your blade quickly forward. Follow through on the shot by extending your bottom hand toward your target and point your stick at it.

To get extra velocity on the shot, press your bottom hand down on

Danny Briere
Wrist-Shot Release

1. Top hand is very close to the body. Wrist is rolled, closing the blade upon release.

2. Bottom hand is a little less than halfway down the shaft. Stick flex is a result of bottom hand pressure through the follow-through. Briere's stick was first flexed with the bow facing the shot. The bow, now facing away from the shot, is an indication of stick whip, which provides velocity to the shot.

3. Briere's right foot lifts from the ice as a result of the torque created by the power and weight that is transferred from the back foot (right foot) to the front foot (left foot).

4. Low follow-through creates a low shot. At the release of his shot, Briere's follow-through will point at his target.

the shaft of the stick (which will cause the stick to flex) just before you release. This flexing will create a whip in the stick that will add a "kick" to the puck upon release.

Tips

✻ Quick hand speed and wrist rolling are very important for a quick release and a fast shot. As in all shots, stick speed is crucial to the speed of your shot.

✻ Your bottom hand should be lower down the shaft of the stick than when stick-handling and passing.

✻ Keeping your hands close to your body as they pass across your body makes it easier to add power to the shot through pressure on the stick, thereby flexing the stick.

✻ The speed of your follow-through will add power to your shot. Extending your bottom hand through the follow-through will allow you to use muscle groups in addition to your arms, like your core and your back, to add power to your shot.

✻ The follow-through can determine the height of your shot.

A high follow-through and an open blade on the follow-through will send the puck higher, while a low follow-through and closed blade will send the puck lower.

✻ If possible, keep your head up throughout the shooting motion, so that you can keep your eye on your target and adjust your shot as needed.

Advanced

Elite players disguise their release of the puck by shooting while puckhandling, often off of their same foot. Alex Ovechkin and Ilya Kovalchuk are particularly good at shooting this way, especially when shooting through a screen on a one-on-one or when they combine the shot with a strong deke to the forehand.

Elite players also learn to change the position of the puck just before releasing it, thus changing the angle of the shot. To do this, either draw the puck in closer to your body before shooting or extend your arms and push the puck away from your body before shooting. For the latter, extend your arms away from your body and move your bottom hand closer to your top hand. You lose a lot of power on this shot, but changing the position of the puck and the angle of the shot can create scoring opportunities. This technique is great when used close to the goal after a deke. The key is to shoot the puck as quickly as possible after you have changed the angle.

Shoot to Score: Tips on Scoring Goals

✻ Practice releasing the puck quickly after receiving a pass, as you might catch the goalie moving. For the quickest release when on your off side, use a one-time snap shot or slap shot off your off foot. When receiving a pass on your proper side, release the puck quickly with a wrist shot off your same foot.

✻ Practice shooting after receiving an off target pass by using the technique on page 88, so that your blade is square on the ice.

✻ Practice spot shooting: hitting a particular spot in the net repeatedly from a particular location on the ice. Some players practice repeatedly shooting stick-side 14 inches off the ice, so that the shot would be over the pad and under the blocker of a butterfly-style goalie.

✻ Try changing the position of the puck, and therefore the angle of the shot, just before releasing the shot. Practice shooting on your forehand or backhand with an extended reach.

✻ A low shot often results in a rebound if it doesn't go in and is very effective when taken on a goalie who is moving his feet, backing in to the net. In close, practice the open bladed shot to get the puck up quickly when the goalie is down.

✻ Shoot through a screen. Moving laterally to cause the defender to turn so they are not square to your shot will open up more areas that you can shoot through.

✻ A shot in motion, particularly off a fake or when driving the net, off your same foot can catch the goaltender moving or not set.

Shooting off of Your Same Foot

This is a deadly way to shoot, and a same-foot shot offers many advantages. You can use this technique many different ways, including: shooting in motion, shooting with a quick release on your proper side, shooting when moving laterally to your proper side and shooting with a deceptive release. The same-foot shot needs to become part of your repertoire.

Vincent Lecavalier

1 Head is up and looking at target; shoulders are square to target. Top hand (which started much closer to the shoulder) is up and ahead of the bottom hand and stick blade, helping to create a slingshot-like whip from the stick.

2 Bottom hand (which is almost straight) is halfway down the shaft and is applying pressure to the shaft (through the heel of the hand) in order to flex the stick and create whip. Both wrists will need to quickly roll the stick blade open and then closed for the wrist-shot release.

3 Body weight is transferred to the same foot by leaning to the same side and lifting the off foot from the ice. This weight transfer applies extra pressure to the stick for extra kick on the shot. The same-side foot is on a flat blade.

In simple terms, your "same" foot is the foot on the same side as the way you shoot—the right foot for right-handed players and the left foot for left-handed players. This is the foot to your "proper" or forehand side. The "off" foot is the foot opposite to the way you shoot—left foot for right-handed players and right foot for left-handed players. This is the foot to your "off" or backhand side.

The traditional way of referring to a player's feet when shooting, namely the "front" and "back" feet, can be confusing. When we refer to the foot that a player shoots off of, we are referring to the foot that the player's weight is on when the shot is released. Many players will shoot from their "off" foot in certain circumstances, and in those circumstances that foot becomes the "front" foot (the foot closest to the target when the puck is released). The wrist shot is a great example of the off foot becoming the front foot. However, the same players will shoot from their "same" foot in other circumstances, when the same foot will become the "front" foot.

Shooting off the same foot is a very effective way of shooting the puck and offers some real advantages over the traditional way of shooting, even on a wrist shot. European players have been using this technique for decades; in fact, during the 1972 Canada-Russia series, announcers and analysts were pointing out that the Russians "didn't even know which foot to shoot off," referring to the fact that the players often shot off their same foot. Now, almost 40 years later, nearly every NHL player can shoot effectively off their same foot, and those who can't are striving to learn how.

Method

To shoot off your same foot, keep your body square to your target with both of your skates facing straight ahead and your head up. With your hands close to your body, bring the puck to your forehand

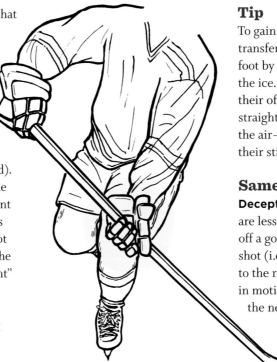

FIG. 59 Front View
A front view of Lecavalier's same-foot shot. Note the body lean and the pressure applied on the middle of the shaft by the nearly straight bottom arm.

side with your stick blade square to your target. When shooting, move all of your weight onto your same foot while applying pressure on your stick, forcing it to flex. Sweep the puck forward with a firm grip. Apply lots of pressure with your bottom hand, and roll your wrists the same as you would for a wrist shot. Follow through after the shot, driving your bottom hand forward and pointing your stick at your target.

Tip

To gain more power on your shot, transfer more weight to your same foot by raising your off foot from the ice. Some players will "kick" their off foot by bending and then straightening their leg—kicking the air—as they put pressure on their stick.

Same Foot Advantages

Deceptive puck release: There are less physical indicators to tip off a goalie as to when to expect a shot (i.e., no weight transfer prior to the release), plus you can shoot in motion (i.e., dekes and drives to the net).

* **Quicker release from passes to your proper wing:** A lefty on the left wing or a righty on the right wing can collect a pass and release it quicker because they don't have to rotate their body and shoot traditionally (transferring weight from the same foot to the off foot).

* **Deceptive off-wing shooting:** With shoulders square to the net, you can draw the puck in close to your body, changing the angle of the shot and concealing the timing of the release.

* **Accuracy:** You can keep your head up throughout the entire shooting motion.

Same-Foot Snap
An aerial view of Viktor Tikhonov taking a same-foot snap shot. The snap shot looks much the same as a same-foot wrist shot, except the puck is not in contact with the stick through the entire shooting motion. By lifting and kicking his off foot, Tikhonov adds pressure to his stick in order to flex it, ultimately giving his shot more kick.

Backhand Shot

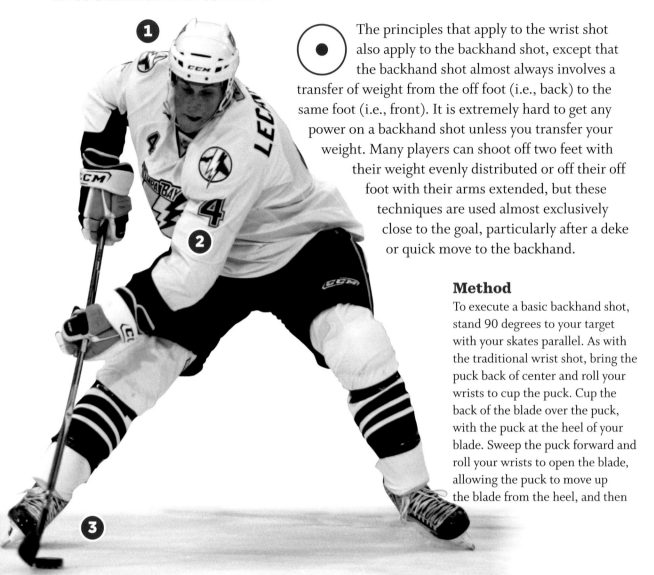

The principles that apply to the wrist shot also apply to the backhand shot, except that the backhand shot almost always involves a transfer of weight from the off foot (i.e., back) to the same foot (i.e., front). It is extremely hard to get any power on a backhand shot unless you transfer your weight. Many players can shoot off two feet with their weight evenly distributed or off their off foot with their arms extended, but these techniques are used almost exclusively close to the goal, particularly after a deke or quick move to the backhand.

Method

To execute a basic backhand shot, stand 90 degrees to your target with your skates parallel. As with the traditional wrist shot, bring the puck back of center and roll your wrists to cup the puck. Cup the back of the blade over the puck, with the puck at the heel of your blade. Sweep the puck forward and roll your wrists to open the blade, allowing the puck to move up the blade from the heel, and then

Vincent Lecavalier

1 Top hand is out from the body, allowing it to move freely across the chest when the puck is swept forward. Wrist is rolled to close the blade over the puck.

2 Left shoulder drops and head is down as the puck is pulled back to begin the shooting motion. Bottom hand pulls the stick through the shooting motion, applying pressure and flexing the stick.

3 Weight is transferred from the back (off) foot to the front (same) foot as the puck is swept forward.

close the blade again before you release the puck. Throughout the movement, transfer your weight from your off foot to your same foot. (The shoulder on your same side will drop a little as you bend your same-side knee to transfer your weight and drive the puck forward.) Concentrate on cradling the puck blade between the heel and center of the closed blade, and release the puck off the middle of your blade. Follow through with a closed blade, drive your bottom hand toward your target and point the blade at your target.

Apply pressure on the shaft of the stick during the release to flex the stick and help whip the puck. Remember to drive the puck using your arms, shoulders and back, not just your wrists. The more open your blade and the higher your follow-through, the higher the puck will go. In order to keep the puck low, keep your blade closed and your follow-through low.

Common Problems

A major mistake made by many players when shooting a backhand is to open the blade on the release in order to flip or lift the puck. This is a good technique to use when you are close to the net but not when shooting from out far. Another common error is to keep the top hand too close to the body when starting the shot. Make sure your top hand is up and away from your body so you can sweep it across your body and maximize the power of your shot.

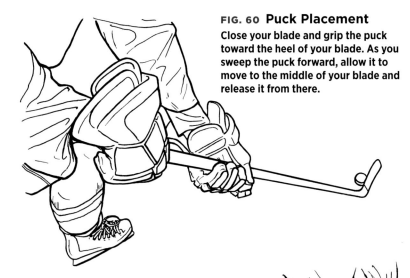

FIG. 60 Puck Placement
Close your blade and grip the puck toward the heel of your blade. As you sweep the puck forward, allow it to move to the middle of your blade and release it from there.

Backhand Advantages

Concealment: When the puck is brought back on the backhand, prior to being released, it can be concealed by the body, which makes it difficult for a goalie to pick up its location. This is particularly true if the drive leg (the front leg) is well bent just before shooting.

Deception: With little indication (other than the angle of the blade) as to where a backhand shot is going, goalies often think that a backhand shot will be high. As a result, if you rotate your hands and close the blade over the puck on the follow-through and shoot the puck low with a low follow-through, it will often surprise a goalkeeper, as the puck will stay closer to the ice.

Top-shelf shooting: When close to the net, it is more natural to shoot the puck with an open blade from the backhand side than it is

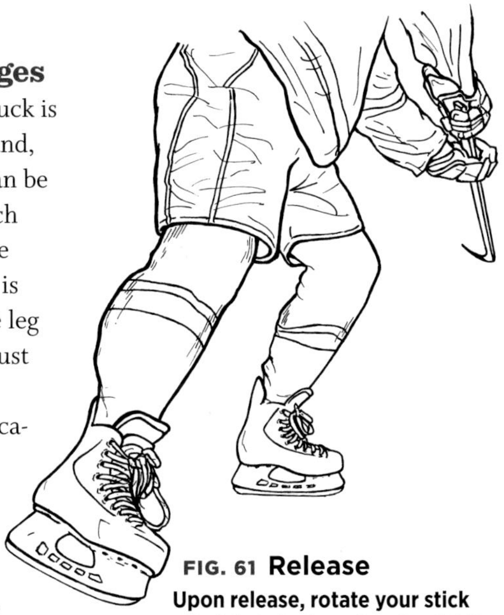

FIG. 61 Release
Upon release, rotate your stick so the blade is closed and point it at your target. A low release will give you a low shot, a high release a high shot. Transfer all of your weight onto your front (same) foot to give the shot as much power as possible.

from the forehand side, making it easier to get the puck up quickly without having to change the position of your body. Deke to the backhand and shoot the puck high!

Snap Shot

A snap shot is your quick-release shot. It is the first shot you'll learn where the blade is not in constant contact with the puck throughout the shooting motion. You don't bring the blade as far back from the puck as you do for a slap shot. Instead, the blade is only brought back a short distance, and sometimes the blade doesn't even leave the ice. A snapshot can be very effective for one-timers from your off wing, off your off foot, or when combined with a toe drag and a change of the angle of the puck.

Jarome Iginla
Snap Shot Release

1 Wrists are rolled to close the blade upon release. Bottom hand is further down the shaft than for a wrist shot, but not as far as it would be for a slap shot. Pressure from the bottom hand flexes the stick, whipping the shot.

2 Bottom arm is extended out and driven hard to propel the snap shot.

FIG. 62 Explosive Release
The key to a snap shot is to quickly explode your stick onto the puck, as you can move your stick faster without the puck than with it. You can still do this while having some contact with the puck: cradle (or drag) the puck with the toe of your stick and then explode onto the puck with the heel of your stick. Release the puck from the middle of the blade.

Technique

The snap shot can be taken from anywhere on your forehand side and can be released traditionally (by moving your weight from back to front), off of your same foot or off of both feet. Once you bring your blade back and away from the puck, immediately explode forward onto the puck, striking it with the middle of your blade and sending it quickly forward.

All in the Wrists

Upon contact, the blade of your stick should be square to the ice; your blade can actually strike the ice just before the puck. When striking the puck, roll your wrists quickly to close your blade then open your blade then go back to a closed blade—the same motion as in a wrist shot. You must roll your wrists extremely quickly as the movement coincides with the blade "moving through" the puck. This is often referred to as "snapping" the puck. Your bottom hand should be slightly lower down on the shaft of the stick than when taking a wrist shot. Grip the stick very tightly with both hands during the shooting motion.

Follow-Through

You can make a snap shot with very little follow-through, relying on a quick stick to explode onto the puck and add speed through the shot, or you can use a strong follow-through similar to the follow-through of a slap shot. When you combine a toe drag movement with a snap shot, you can use a strong follow-through, similar to a wrist shot, to provide speed and accuracy to your shot. The height of your follow-through determines the height of your shot.

Snap Shot vs. Wrist Shot

The snap shot is a very effective quick-release shot, particularly when shooting on your off wing or shooting a pass from your forehand side. A snap shot is also effective as a quick-release shot off of your same foot or off of both feet. The advantage of taking a snap shot over a wrist shot is that you can increase your stick speed—you can move the stick faster without the puck than with it. This means that you can move the stick at a higher speed through the shooting motion, increasing the speed of your shot. The disadvantage is that a snap shot is not as accurate as a wrist shot, as you might not strike the puck in the middle of the blade or have the blade square with the puck upon contact. This is particularly true if you keep your head up throughout the shooting motion.

Combination Wrist Shot–Snap Shot

You can use this shot to change the position of the puck prior to your shot. It also disguises the snap shot. The set up for this shot is the same as for a traditional wrist shot, but you use a snap-shot release.

First change the position of the puck by pulling it toward your body. Bring the middle and heel of the blade up and back from the puck while keeping the toe of the stick on the ice. To release the puck, drive the middle and heel of the blade forward and snap the puck. This shot can be made from the off or same foot. Mark Messier shot the puck very effectively on his off wing using this technique.

Slap Shot

A slap shot can be devastatingly hard and fast, but it can also take a while to release and is often a shooter's least accurate shot. However, if you can harness the strength of the slap shot, it can be deadly.

Executing a slap shot is similar to releasing a snap shot, except you need to bring the stick back farther before contacting the puck, your bottom hand needs to be lower on the shaft of the stick and your follow-through is much more pronounced.

Method

To start, position yourself with your feet 90 degrees to your target and place the puck in the middle of your body but slightly toward your front foot. The backswing of a slap shot can vary from a shorter "half" backswing, which stays parallel to the ice, to a full backswing, in which the stick is raised much higher and is almost vertical. During the backswing, rotate your hands as you would when drawing the blade back just before releasing a snap shot, and place your bottom hand slightly lower down on the shaft of the stick than when taking a snap shot. Ensure the blade is closed over the puck when it makes contact with it, and snap your wrists when you release. Strike the puck with the middle of the blade and ensure the blade is square to the ice. Your stick should strike the ice just behind the puck. Be sure to keep the puck close enough to your body so that you can place full pressure on the shaft of the stick with your bottom hand. This pressure will flex and whip the stick, which will help propel the puck.

Alex Ovechkin Slap-Shot Release

1 Bottom hand has slid up the shaft of the stick as the torque from the shot twists Ovechkin's body. During the shot, the bottom hand would have been up to 12 inches further down the shaft (see page 18). In order to properly follow through, Ovechkin loosened his bottom-hand grip after shooting. If he didn't slide his bottom hand up the shaft after shooting,

his shoulder would over rotate and cause him to twist too far, likely making him fall.

2 Blade is closed and pointing at the target. The higher the follow-through, the higher the shot.

3 Weight is transferred from back leg to front leg. The back leg is lifted to apply more weight to the transfer. It is also lifted because of the amount of torque the shooting motion generated.

Follow-Through

The entire motion should be completed very quickly, as stick speed will affect the speed of your shot; make sure you transfer your weight from your back foot to your front foot quickly. A strong follow-through is also important and allows you to use your hips, back, shoulders and arms during the shot. You should follow through until your bottom hand is driven almost straight ahead,

FIG. 63 Backswing
Your backswing can be small (low to the ice), medium (as illustrated here), or large (stick straight up in the air) depending on the amount of time you have. Regardless of your backswing type, be sure to load as much energy and weight onto your back foot as you can so that you can transfer that into your shot when you follow through to your front foot.

with the stick pointing at your target. As you drive your weight forward and follow through on the shot, your back leg may want to come up off the ice. This can add power to your shot by adding weight to the transfer that happens from back to front, and it also gives you more torque on the shot and a full extension of your arms on the follow-through. However, ending a slap shot on one foot requires great balance, as your body is moving forward and twisting with a great deal of power.

Most players need to drop their head and look at the puck when shooting a slap shot. This allows them to see if they are striking the puck properly, but it also means that the shot may be less accurate. As your slap shot improves, try to keep your head up throughout the shooting motion. This will allow you to be more accurate; it will also enable you to change from a slap shot to a slap pass if the situation on the ice calls for it. Wayne Gretzky may have been the first player to use the "heads up" slap shot effectively.

Tip

The slap shot is very effective for one-time shots, particularly when you are on your off wing. A fake slap shot can also be very effective (see page 111). Players can drive off the fake and shoot while in motion or move the puck to a player who is in a better position to score a goal.

Slap Pass

Vincent Lecavalier is executing a head-up slap pass. A slap pass is a great fake. As if executing a slap shot, Lecavalier has his hand down low on the shaft, but look closer and you'll see his stick flexion is non-existent and his shoulders are square to a direction separate from where he is looking.

Open-Bladed Shot

The best shot to use when close to the goalie is the open-bladed shot, as it enables a player to get the puck up and over the goalkeeper quickly, which is very important since goalkeepers are becoming increasingly better at covering the lower parts of the net. This shot can also be used when you need to get the puck up quickly, such as to clear the puck out of the defensive zone or dump it into the offensive zone.

You can execute an open-bladed shot with a traditional release (standing 90 degrees to the target with your skates parallel) or by shooting off of your same foot. It can be used on your forehand side or your backhand side. The key to a successful open-bladed shot is to rotate your hands so the blade is open while you are shooting. When the blade is open you can use a wrist-shot shooting motion to "wrist," or scoop, the puck up with the middle of your blade. You can also use a snap-shot motion, snapping the puck off the heel, middle or toe of the front of your blade. In either case, the shooting motion will start in closer to your body than with a regular wrist or snap shot. To help get the puck closer to your body, you need to move your top hand away from your body and your bottom hand down low on the shaft of your stick and bring your follow-through up high. This will enable you to shoot the puck up high very quickly. This shooting technique is very effective for scoring when close to the goalie. Johan Franzen and Tomas Holmstrom are two NHLers who are very good at scoring goals with this shot.

Brad Richards
Open-Bladed Snap

1 Top hand is out and away from the body so that Richards can bring the puck in closer to his body.

2 Bottom hand is down low on the shaft so the puck can be brought in closer to his body, and so he can quickly get underneath the puck with either a scooping-type wrist shot or a snap shot.

3 Blade will move rapidly onto the puck with a snap-shot motion on the heel, middle or toe of the front of the blade.

7

Dekeing and Deception

Ilya Kovalchuk attempts to move the puck through a defender to a position on the other side of the defender where he can retrieve it. See page 119 for more on moving pucks through defenders.

Off-Foot Fake Shots

The easiest and most effective deke for you to learn when shooting from your off foot (the front foot in a traditional shooting setup) is to fake a shot then move to your forehand. Moving to your forehand allows you to accelerate easily off the fake, and it allows you to pass or shoot on your forehand immediately after the fake as the puck remains in a shooting or passing position throughout. When faking a shot it is important to imitate the shooting motion as closely as possible; the defender has to believe you are going to shoot the puck in order for the fake to work. The fake shots in this section will all be followed by a move to the forehand.

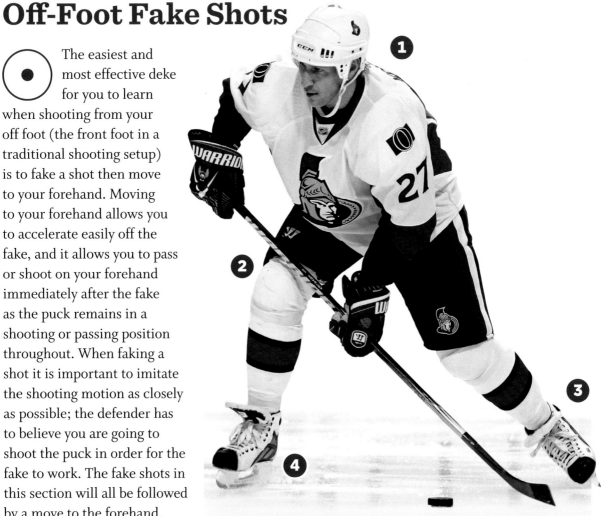

Alex Kovalev
Fake Slap Shot

1 Head is up and eyes are looking at the target to help sell the fake.

2 Bottom hand is down low on the shaft to help sell the shot, but not so low that it will hinder the attack off the fake to the forehand side. Once Kovalev's stick reaches the puck he will move his top hand further away from his body and rotate his wrists to turn his blade so he can push the puck to his forehand side off the fake.

3 Back foot is kept close to the ice as Kovalev begins to bring it underneath his body toward his front foot. Once his feet touch underneath his body, Kovalev's back foot will become the lead skate for the initial drive to the forehand.

4 Toe of Kovalev's front foot has begun rotating to his off side in preparation for the drive off the fake to his forehand side.

Fake Slap Shot

This is the easiest fake shot to learn. While effective on its own, it is also a stepping-stone that will help you learn more challenging dekes and learn to move laterally to your forehand off a fake.

To sell the shot, bring your stick back to initiate the slap-shot motion. Move your stick quickly through the shooting motion, moving your hands across and in toward your body as the blade moves toward the puck. Simultaneously bring your same foot (back foot) under your body and toward your off foot. Keep your same foot close to the ice. Progressively bend both of your knees and bring your same foot underneath your body to touch your off foot. When your stick blade reaches the puck, stop the forward motion of your hands: push your top hand away from your body and bring your bottom hand into your body while rolling your wrists to rotate the stick blade so it is open and facing your forehand side. The puck will be on your forehand side and your blade will be facing the direction you are going to drive off the fake, not the original direction of your "shot." Take a full stride to your forehand side, driving from your off foot and leading with your same foot. The angle on which you accelerate to beat the defender or create space will depend on many factors, including your speed and the positioning and reaction of the defender.

FIG. 64

Fake Slap-Shot Windup

Wind up for your fake shot as you would for a regular slap shot, but keep in mind that the longer your stick is in the air behind you, the more time you are giving to defenders to close the gap on you. A short to medium backswing is best.

Fake Snap Shot

You sell a fake off-foot snap shot by going through exactly the same motions you do for a fake slap shot, except your backswing for the snap shot is not as large. This makes the fake snap shot less pronounced than the fake slap shot, and in order to effectively sell the snap shot you need to exaggerate the body and hand movements outlined for the fake slap shot (but with a smaller backswing). It also means that you don't have as much time to bring your same foot underneath you in order to set up your drive off the fake, so you need to be very quick.

You can also fake a snap shot by keeping your stick blade on the ice. This fake is subtler and again requires that you exaggerate your body and hand movements to sell the shot. Your foot and hand movements are the same as those previously described. However, your stick movement at the outset of the fake snap shot is different.

Start with the puck out slightly ahead of you on your forehand side and extend your reach. Fake the snap shot by rolling your wrists to

FIG. 65 Drive off the Fake

As your stick blade nears the puck (the point just before you would release it if you were shooting), rotate your wrists, push your top hand out and turn your blade to face your forehand side. Lean into the drive and push to your forehand side with your off foot (the front foot in your original shooting motion).

lift the heel of your stick off the ice and, with the toe of your stick, drag the puck in toward your body. As you drag the puck in toward your body, roll your wrists in the opposite direction so that the heel of your stick returns to the ice. You'll need to move your top hand out and away from your body as your same foot comes underneath you in preparation for your lateral drive to your forehand, just as you do during the fake slap shot. When you are in this position, which looks identical to the position of the fake slap shot, take a full stride to your forehand, driving off your off foot and leading with your same foot. This fake can be very effective because the puck moves quite a bit through the shooting motion, an extra element the defender needs to read.

Fake Wrist Shot

The movement for this fake is the subtlest of all the off-foot fake shots, and it requires you commit

FIG. 66 & 67 Snap-Shot Fake to Forehand Drive

Start with the puck on your forehand side out from your body. With a toe drag, cradle the puck and drag it toward your feet with the heel of your stick in the air. Have your eyes up looking at your "shot target." Simultaneously bring your same-side foot underneath your body, beside your off foot. Rotate your wrists, push your top hand out and turn your blade to face your forehand side. Lean into the drive and push to your forehand side with your off foot.

Notes on Fake Shots

Keys to the Forehand Drive off the Fake

Once you fake a shot you are in position to accelerate off the fake, but be quick, as the window of opportunity is small. After your initial drive—pushing from your off foot and leading with your same leg—you must accelerate using cross-overs and drive around your opponent into open space. Your drive can lead you to the net or, against good defenders who adjust to the fake quickly, you can use a drive and delay to create space. You can also shoot or pass off the fake before the defender has time to either adjust and fill the shooting lane or get a stick on your stick as you are shooting.

To Shoot or Not to Shoot

With all fake shots, you can wait to decide whether or not to shoot until just before the point of release. This will help you "sell" your shot, since you can actually be in the process of shooting then decide that it will be to your advantage—due to the positioning of the defender or the goalie or other factors—to fake the shot instead.

Using Fake Shots to Change Angles

Faking a shot (or even just hesitating while in a shooting position) in order to freeze the defender or goalie, or to have the defender or goalie commit to the fake, is a great play, giving you time and space to make a play or to move the puck to a different shooting position.

to exaggerating the movements of your wrist shot.

The same general technique used for the fake slap shot is used for the fake wrist shot, except the puck remains on your stick at all times. Sell the fake by bringing the puck back as you would for a wrist shot and then quickly bring it forward as though you are going to release the shot. As you bring the puck forward on your fake shot, bring your hands into your body. As you reach what would ordinarily be the point of release, push your top hand out and away from your body and bring your bottom hand into your body while rolling your wrists to rotate the stick blade so it is open and facing your forehand side—the same way you would for the fake slap shot and the fake snap shot. As with the slap-shot and snap-shot fakes, you need to simultaneously bring your same foot underneath you and toward your off foot so you can quickly drive off your fake to the forehand.

If you start your fake wrist shot with the puck away from your body, you can use a toe drag to keep the puck on your stick and move your hands into your body to begin setting up the drive—same as you would a fake snap shot.

The real challenge of the fake wrist shot is to bring the puck forward quickly enough to sell the shot and then slow the puck down, rotate your top hand and quickly drive laterally to your forehand side while keeping the puck under control the entire time.

The key to changing the angle or shooting position is to move the puck from the release position of the "intended" shot to the new shooting position as quickly as possible before releasing the puck. Your new shooting position may mean moving the puck a short distance or a long distance, but either way it will change the angle of the shot. In order to release the shot as quickly as possible, you may need to shoot off an extended reach, either on your backhand or your forehand side, or you may need to shoot from a position with the puck drawn into your body.

You can effectively use many different shots off this fake, and because so many goalies are very good at covering the bottom of the net while moving laterally, it is to your advantage to put the puck high after moving it to your new shooting point. This fake is effective whether you are in close to the goalie or farther out. The open-bladed shot (see page 107), which allows you to get the puck up quickly, is particularly effective in this situation. If you want to keep the puck low to the ice, try a low, hard shot to the five-hole, as many goalies open up their five-hole when they move laterally to adjust to the change in the shooting angle. If you have used your fake in close to the goalkeeper, your best option may be to shoot with one hand off an extended reach. This will often result in a tap-in after you have moved the puck back against the direction in which both you and the goalie are traveling (see the Forsberg move, page 136). Changing your shooting angle is a very effective move on breakaways and shootouts.

Double Fakes

A double fake can create open space, but it requires room, as you need to fake a shot and then fake a drive to your forehand side, only to come back and drive around the defender to your backhand side. To do this, fake a shot and drive to your forehand side as outlined on page 111. Once you have begun your forehand drive, quickly move the puck across your body toward your backhand side. Continue pushing the puck to your backhand side while extending your reach and using cross-overs to accelerate into a backhand drive. The key is to use the momentum you gained from your first fake to accelerate into the drive for your second fake. Remember to start your first fake earlier to give yourself more space between you and the defender in order to execute the two fakes.

Same-Foot Fake Shots

Same-foot fakes have become much more common as the use of same-foot shots has increased. If you are faking a wrist shot or snap shot off your same foot, or off both of your feet, you can move effectively to your forehand or to your backhand off the fake.

Rick Nash

1 Stick is held in a shooting stance, making Nash a threat to shoot at any time during the fake.

2 Same-side foot is on its inside edge, about to drive to his off side.

3 Off-foot is returning to the ice, heel first, from the same-foot shot position. The heel-first position will slow Nash down and allow him to turn to his off side. From here he can drive to his backhand while he continues to travel to his off side, or he can cut back to his same side—a double fake.

Method

To sell a same-foot fake, set up as if you are going to take the shot. Lean your body to your same side and apply lots of pressure to the shaft of your stick with your bottom hand. Raise, or raise and kick, your off foot, as this gives the impression that you have committed to the shot.

In most cases, in order to move to your forehand or backhand side off the fake, you have to bring your off foot back down on the ice. However, the split-second hesitation that raising your foot can buy you is often enough to get a defender or the goalie out of position long enough for you to capitalize on their mistake. Once you have frozen the defending player, you can put your off foot down and attack laterally on your forehand or backhand side. It is also very effective to hesitate in the shooting position after you have brought your off foot back onto the ice and are still square to the defender or goalie. This gives you a second opportunity to freeze the defending player and may buy you more time to execute your move to your backhand or forehand side. Any time you have pressure on your stick with your blade facing a target and your shoulders square to the net, you are a threat to shoot.

Tip

✳ Use the fake off-foot shot as a fake dump-in to create space in front of you. For example, if you are attacking a defender through the neutral zone on your off wing, the fake dump-in off your same foot may cause the defender to back off a little, giving you more space to work. Marian Hossa uses this move effectively.

Same-Foot Fake to Change the Angle

It is possible to deke to your forehand side before you put your off foot onto the ice, but you should not use this fake to get around an opponent; instead, you should use it to change the angle of your shot or pass. To execute this fake, raise your off foot from the ice as you would for a same-foot shot. Once you are in this position, begin to turn toward your forehand side by using the outside edge of your same skate—lean in slightly toward the puck using your stick for balance. To give yourself a boost of speed, pump the knee of your off leg (which is already in the air) by thrusting it up and into your body. This will propel you on your same foot toward your forehand side. Once you have changed the angle, look to quickly shoot or pass the puck. Keith Tkachuk has used this fake very effectively.

FIG. 68 & 69 Changing the Angle of Attack

Fake a same-foot shot and hold the fake as long as you can in order to freeze the defender. Lean slightly toward your same side and use the outside edge of your same-side blade to turn toward your forehand side, giving you a new angle to shoot or pass the puck. To execute the move with speed, pump your off-side knee as you turn toward your forehand side.

Fake Backhand Shot

Like a slap shot or wrist shot, you can fake a backhand shot and move off the fake to a forehand position for a shot, a pass or a drive into open space. One difficulty with the fake backhand is that in selling the backhand shot you have to drop your head just before the "shot," making yourself vulnerable to a defender who might step up to make contact. It is important to give yourself enough space from the defender when you initiate the fake and to move quickly between the shooting fake and the forehand position.

Set up the fake backhand shot as you would a real backhand, with your same side closest to the target. Have your stick blade square to the target and back of center with the puck cradled on the back of your blade. Lower your same-side shoulder to further sell the shot, and if safe to do so, drop your head. Sweep your hands forward as you would if you were releasing the shot, but instead, bring your hands in toward and across your body to your forehand side, keeping the puck on the back of your blade. Simultaneously drive from the inside edge of your off foot and the outside edge of your same foot to rotate your feet with your body. The motion of your stick, body and feet is very similar to executing a tight turn on your backhand. Once you have turned to your forehand side, lift your stick blade over the puck to the front of your blade so you are ready to shoot or pass on the forehand.

This can be a great fake on a goaltender, especially when combined with a move back to your backhand after initially faking the backhand shot and moving to your forehand (a double fake). Make sure you give yourself extra room to execute the two moves.

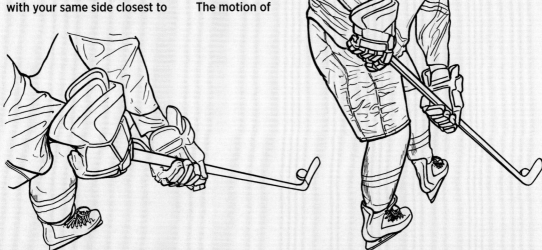

FIG. 70 Fake Backhand Setup
Place the puck behind your off foot, the same way you would if you were setting up a backhand shot. To help sell the shot, drop your same-side shoulder and, if it is safe to do so, you can briefly drop your head.

FIG. 71 Transition from Shot to Turn
Sweep the puck forward and drive from the inside edge of your off foot and the outside edge of your same foot to initiate a tight turn. Cup the puck on the back of your blade and in close to your feet to avoid stick checks. Progress through the turn, and once on your forehand side, lift your stick over the puck so that it is on the forehand side of your stick blade.

Lateral Attack Moves

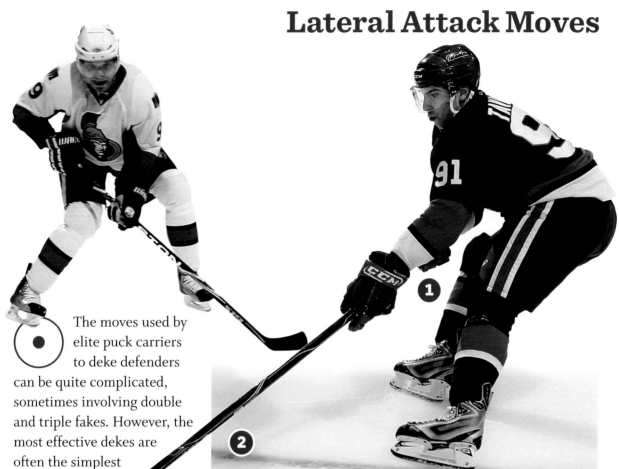

The moves used by elite puck carriers to deke defenders can be quite complicated, sometimes involving double and triple fakes. However, the most effective dekes are often the simplest ones, such as the lateral attack, which involves faking to either your forehand or backhand side, quickly moving the puck across your body to the opposite side, then quickly driving around the defender in this new direction. Lateral attacks are most effective when you accelerate off the fake so the fake is combined with a change of speed to separate yourself from the defender.

John Tavares
Fake to the Forehand, Toe Drag to Middle, Lateral Attack to the Forehand

1 Bottom hand is high on the shaft near the top hand to extend the puck out to the forehand side. Hands are low to the ice and upper body is bent to maximize the extension.

2 Heel of the blade is slightly off the ice, and the puck is cupped with the toe of the blade. Tavares will toe drag the puck toward and into his body. At the same time, he will bring his same skate underneath his body to touch his off skate. He will then move his top hand away from his body and rotate his stick blade to push the puck back out to his forehand side (like the drive off a fake shot—see page 111). He will drive back to his forehand and around the defender with a drive from his off skate, and he will lead with his same skate as he accelerates.

117

Lateral Attack to the Forehand

A lateral attack to your forehand side allows you to have two hands on your stick at all times and the puck on your forehand after the fake, which is a great advantage because you will have the puck in a shooting or passing position. At its simplest, this move is a fake drive on your backhand side with a quick movement of the puck across your body to your forehand side followed by a drive to your forehand.

The first and most important step is to sell your fake backhand-side drive. Mimic driving to your backhand by extending your reach with the puck to your backhand side. When you extend the puck to your backhand side, do so at a 45-degree angle forward, so the puck is still close to you but has also moved closer to the defender (as it would if you were really attacking to your backhand side). Remember that the more you extend the puck away from your body, the further it has to come back and across your body—and the more time and space you need to execute the move. Against players who are focused on playing close to your body it may be better to use a shorter, quicker fake and to extend the puck a shorter distance to your backhand side. The key is to appear to be starting to drive to your backhand side.

Bend your off knee as you extend your reach to your backhand side;

this will allow you to drive off your off skate for your forehand attack. When you are ready to execute your forehand attack, bring your same foot underneath you, toward your off foot. Keep your same foot close to the ice. When your same foot meets your off foot, angle your same foot in the direction you want to drive and push off your off foot. Simultaneously bring your hands from your backhand side to your forehand side. Bring your hands across your body, and then push them out, away from your body, to your forehand side by extending your reach. As you move the puck across your body to your forehand side, cup the puck with the back of your blade. You may need to draw the puck in toward your body to keep it out of the defender's reach before you push it out to your forehand side with the front of your blade. It is important that you extend the puck to your forehand first and that your body follows.

After your first full stride to your forehand side—driving off your off foot with your same foot leading—continue to accelerate around the defender using cross-overs. Even if you don't need to accelerate after moving to your forehand, such as when you are faking on a goalie, it is still good to bring your same foot underneath you before you drive off the fake as you will have the option to move in any direction when both of your feet are underneath you.

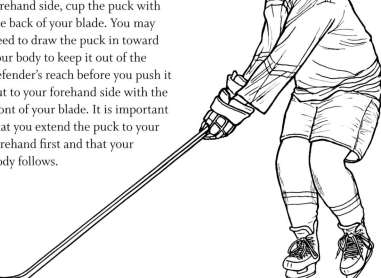

FIG. 72 Fake to the Backhand to Lateral Attack to the Forehand
Extend your reach and present the puck to the your backhand side. When you decide to attack to the forehand, bend your knees and bring your same-side foot toward your off-side foot. As you bring the puck toward the middle of your body and push it back out on the forehand side, drive to your forehand side off the inside edge of your off foot; use your same-side foot to lead the drive and then glide. Lead your forehand attack with the puck first and your feet second.

Lateral Attack to the Backhand

Apply the principles of a lateral attack to your forehand side to a lateral attack to your backhand side, except you need to mirror the attack: for the lateral attack to your backhand you need to fake a forehand drive, move the puck across the defender and drive to your backhand side.

Your fake forehand drive can be short or extended—the more extended the forehand fake, the better you can sell it to the defender, but the longer it takes you to bring the puck back across your body. The forehand fake is

Moving Pucks Through Defenders

Pavel Datsyuk has faked a backhand drive and has extended his reach with only his top hand on his stick. He will pass the puck underneath Ryan Suter's stick before driving off the inside edge of his off skate to move to his forehand, around Suter.

Options off of Lateral Attacks

Shooting in Motion Through Defenders

∗ Turn defenders into a screen and shoot "through" them after the fake while you're moving off the drive. If the defender turns to cover you on the drive and is able to stay with you, you can release your shot through the defender, as there will be more openings through his or her body or under his or her stick as the defender is no longer square to the puck. With both you and the defender moving when you take the shot, it can become a challenge for the goalie to find the puck through the moving screen. In addition, you are releasing the puck in motion off a fake. Alex Ovechkin does this very effectively.

Sliding the Puck Across Your Body and Through a Defender

∗ When executing this move you engage defenders so much with your fake drive that they turn to defend the fake, opening up and allowing you to move the puck through them. The key to this move is to sell the fake drive by accelerating into it. You can use two hands on your stick to your forehand or backhand side, but using one hand and extending your reach to your backhand side might result in the defender "chasing" the puck and being pulled further out of position with the fake. Once the defender has turned to react to the fake drive and is closing in on you, bring the puck, with one or two hands, across your body and through holes in the defender's body (between the feet or through the opening between the defender's stick blade and body). When working your way across the defender's body, depending on how close the check is, you may find you need to draw the puck in toward your body to avoid the puck hitting the defender. Ideally, you will be able to retrieve the puck on the other side of the defender and then drive around the defender.

usually done with two hands on the stick, and it is effective when you take a few strides to your forehand to sell the fake. Make sure to bend your same-side knee when extending your reach to your forehand side. This will help you sell the fake, and it will allow you to push off your same leg when you drive to your backhand side.

When you are ready to execute your backhand attack, bring your off foot in toward your same foot and angle it in the direction you want to travel. Keep your off foot close to the ice and drive off your same foot and lead with your off foot. At the same time, bring the puck across your body from your forehand side using the front of your blade while pulling it in toward your body. This will allow you to keep it away from the defender before you push it out to your backhand side with the front of your blade.

You can now drive to your backhand side with the puck on the back of the blade. Extend your reach with the puck by moving it away from your body—and the defender—with one hand (or two hands) on your stick while using cross-overs to accelerate past the defender. The key to this deke, whether using one hand or two, is to move the puck first and then accelerate with cross-overs. If you accelerate during the extension of the puck you will advance on the defender too quickly, allowing the defender to close the gap, giving you less space.

Lateral Attack with a Heel Turn

During this move you use pressure on the inside edge of the heel of your skate like a brake or rudder to steer you in a different direction.

Unlike the lateral attack to the forehand or backhand, your skates are in a wider stance and stay on the ice. By putting pressure on the inside edge of the heel of one of your skates you will slow yourself down, your momentum will turn your body, and your other foot will turn quickly toward the direction of the skate that is acting like a rudder. Therefore, applying pressure to your right heel will turn your body to the right, and applying pressure with your left heel will turn you left. To put the most pressure on your heels, lift the front part of your skate off the ice.

Combine a heel turn with the same fakes and puck movements as a lateral attack: fake to the side that you will be turning away from, and bring the puck across your body to the other side, the side that you are turning toward. Remember to bring the puck in toward your body as you bring it across your body to avoid a stick check. The biggest difference between a lateral attack with a heel turn and a traditional

lateral attack is that the change of speed that accompanies the change of direction involves deceleration as opposed to acceleration.

A lateral attack with a heel turn is very effective when you need to slow down then quickly change direction on a defender or goalie. A good example would be if you have accelerated toward a defender who has backed into the net and you want to move around the defender quickly to shoot without getting too close to the goalie. Another good opportunity to use a heel turn is when you want to decelerate and

Keys to Lateral Attacks

Sell the fake. Imitate the original movement as closely as possible: use your body and stick placement, as well as your eyes, to sell the fake. Footwork, including aggressive skating into and off the fake, helps as well.

Quickly bring the puck across your body after the initial fake, before the defender has time to react, and drive in the opposite direction.

Bring the puck in toward you and away from the defender while moving it across your body. This allows you to avoid stick-on-stick checks by defenders while getting even closer to them when executing attacks, giving them less time to adjust and giving you a more direct line to the net.

Extend your reach when going around the defender. Extend your arms, bend your knees, bring your hands close together at the top of your stick and rotate your wrists to cup and protect the puck. This will allow you to keep the puck away from a checking defender during the initial fake and the drive off the fake.

Heel Turn

Dan Boyle drives the heel of his off foot into the ice as he moves to his backhand on a breakaway against Marty Turco. Boyle's left heel acts as a break and a rudder. With his momentum toward the net, his right foot will turn toward his off side. The heel turn is a very effective way to slow your forward movement and turn sharply. This will allow you to move laterally and stay away from the net so that you can get the puck up over a goalie who has gone down.

move laterally on a breakaway in order to stay out from the goalie and put the puck up high. The move also works extremely well in confined spaces. As with any lateral attack move, when you're in close to a defender or goalie a fake can create openings in a defender that you can move the puck through—either as a shot, a pass or a pass to yourself.

When you execute a heel turn in open ice it is very important to use forward cross-overs to drive around your opponent after the heel turn to regain your speed.

Toe Drags

A toe drag, particularly the forehand toe drag, is one of the most commonly used vertical dekes. The goal is to push the puck out, away from your body, then bring it back in. When executed properly, the toe drag allows you to move the puck a great distance from your body (enticing defenders to take the bait) before drawing it back into your body to protect it. Toe drags are very effective when coupled with lateral attack moves.

Forehand Toe Drag

To beat defenders with a forehand toe drag you must first convincingly present the puck to them. Your goal is to change the position of the puck to such an extent that defenders commit to the new puck position. They may believe the puck is vulnerable and may adjust their body position in order to reach the puck. Once the defender commits you can pull the puck back and drive to open space.

Begin by pushing the puck away from your body, either in front of you or to your forehand side, while executing a forehand attack (lateral or straight ahead). When the defender reacts to the presentation

of the puck, pull the puck back by dragging it toward you with the inside toe of your stick blade, which should be almost square to the ice; the heel of your stick should be in the air, and the back of your blade should be facing the defender. For extra control on the drag, place your thumb on the side of your stick's shaft. Next draw your hands in toward your body to pull the puck back. You can then drive around the defender, either by moving the puck across your body to your backhand side where you can execute a lateral attack to your backhand or moving back to your forehand with a lateral attack to your forehand side.

Rob Schremp
Forehand Toe Drag

Rob Schremp does a forehand toe drag to elude Tampa defenseman Matt Smaby.

1 Schremp has the puck on the toe of his blade as he begins to drag it back toward himself.

2 His bottom hand is very loose as he rotates the shaft of his stick to bring the toe of his blade squarer to the ice and the heel of his blade further into the air. Once his shaft is rotated, his bottom-hand grip will become tighter in order to pull the puck into his body.

3 With his off foot in the air and his body leaning to his off side, Schremp may attempt a backhand drive after the toe drag, or he could fake the backhand drive and come back to the forehand side to attack. Schremp may need to straighten his body as he drags the puck back in order to keep it as far away as possible from Smaby's stick.

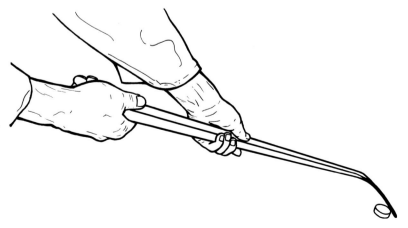

FIG. 73 Hand Position for the Forehand Toe Drag
With the puck at the inside of the toe of your blade, rotate your hands so the toe of your blade becomes squarer to the ice and the heel is in the air. The back of your blade should face your opponent. Place your thumbs on the side of the shaft for better control as you drag the puck back.

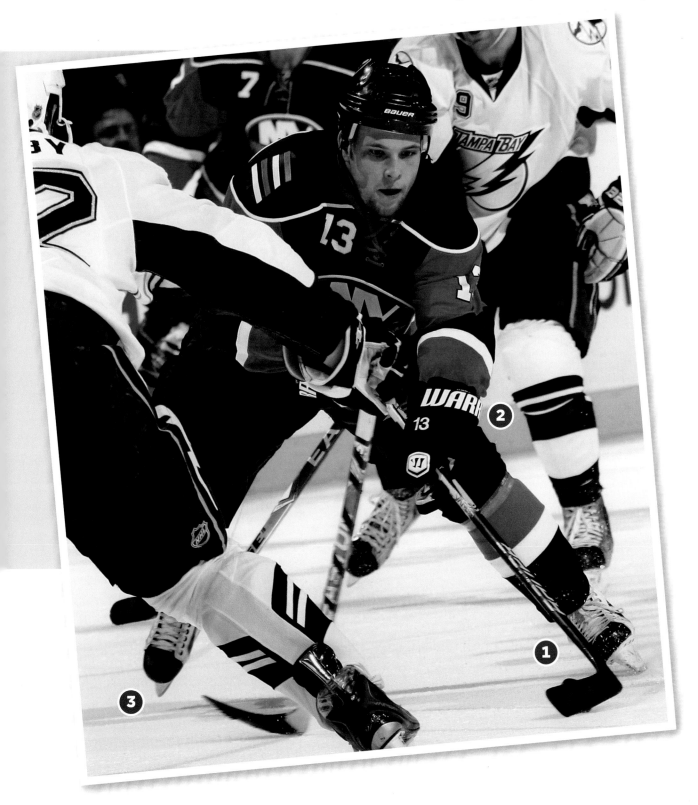

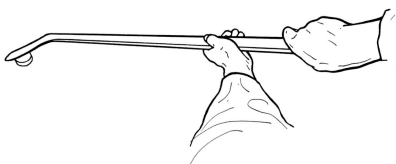

FIG. 74 Hand Position for the Backhand Toe Drag
With the puck at the outside toe of your blade, rotate your hands so that the toe of your blade becomes squarer to the ice and the heel is in the air. The front of your blade should face your opponent. Place your thumb on the side of the shaft for better control as you drag the puck back.

To drive to your forehand side off a forehand toe drag, bring your same foot underneath you as you draw the puck toward your body, then drive off your off foot while extending your reach to your forehand side, just as you would during the lateral attack to your forehand.

Regardless of whether you choose to attack to your backhand or forehand side, you will want to bring your feet underneath you to allow for an effective drive and a good first stride into the lateral attack.

Backhand Toe Drag

For the backhand toe drag, extend your reach and present the puck to the defender on your backhand side. With both hands on your stick, drag the puck in toward your body with the toe of the back of your stick blade, which should be almost square to the ice. The heel of your stick should be in the air, and the front of the blade should be facing the defender.

As you are pulling the puck in, set yourself up for a drive around the defender. You can move the puck from your backhand side

across your body to your same side for a forehand drive, or you can go back to your off side for a backhand drive. Remember to bring your feet together for an effective drive and a good first stride to the lateral attack.

One-Handed Backhand Toe Drag

The same principles that apply to conventional two-handed drags—present the puck then drag it back and drive around the defender—apply to the one-handed backhand toe drag, except that you are presenting the puck and dragging it back with only your top hand on your stick.

Extend your reach with the puck with one hand on your stick and present it toward your backhand side. Keep your top hand and arm raised while you extend your reach to control the puck. When the defender reacts to the presentation of the puck, drag it in toward you with the backhand-side toe of your stick's blade.

You'll find it easier to drive around the defender if you sell the one-handed backhand toe drag as a backhand lateral attack move. Start by accelerating to your backhand side with one hand on your stick, and sell the defender on your intention to continue this drive. Once the defender has committed to this path, decelerate and draw the puck back with a one-handed backhand toe drag. At this point you can bring the puck across your body to your forehand side

FIG. 75 One-Handed Backhand Toe Drag

With one hand on your stick, practice extending your reach to the backhand with the puck, toe dragging the puck back to your backhand side, and pushing the puck back out again. Your wrist should roll more than 180 degrees from your extension to your toe drag, to the puck at your side. Remember to always keep your hand up in order to have your stick blade (and toe during the drag) square to the ice.

and drive around the defender to your forehand, or you can drag the puck back and drive again to your backhand side.

To drive back to your backhand side, drag the puck in toward you with the backhand-side toe of your stick's blade. As the puck moves toward you, the back of your stick blade will be facing you and your palm will be facing down. Once you bring your top hand into your body, rotate your top hand so that your palm is facing up and your stick blade moves between you and the puck. The puck will still be on the back of your blade. Next, quickly push the puck ahead of you and to your backhand side with the back of your blade. Accelerate and continue the drive to your backhand side. This option can get defenders tied up, and it should give you enough room after the toe drag to beat the player to the backhand.

Keys to the Toe Drag

Toe drags often work well with an acceleration to set them up and then a deceleration as the drag is being executed. Extending your arms just before you slow down will make your presentation of the puck more pronounced and give you more room to drag the puck back. The idea is to accelerate forward with the puck and then decelerate while extending your reach, which you use to continue the forward movement of the puck even though you have stopped skating forward. This will disguise your deceleration, making it more likely for the defender to be caught out of position. Some players have had success with this move when on their proper side on a one-on-one or a two-on-one. In this instance, the defender will angle toward the puck carrier hoping to block a shot or pass. The puck carrier can use deceleration combined with a toe drag to change the angle of attack, leaving the defender out of position and creating space for a shot or a pass.

Skate Moves

Skate moves—playing the puck off your skate and then back to your stick—can be an important part of your deception repertoire. At the same time, it is crucial that you avoid doing a skate move just for the sake of it and only use the skill to accomplish something significant on the ice. Performing a skate move is often a risky play during which you could lose the puck or put yourself in a vulnerable position to be checked. However, some skate moves can be executed with a higher percentage of success, particularly with practice. There are many different possibilities when it comes to skate moves, and while skate moves are not commonly used, they can be very effective in the right situation.

Vincent Lecavalier

1 Head is up and looking for a potential cross-ice pass. As long as the puck is on the front of the stick blade to the forehand side, Lecavalier is a threat to shoot or pass. Faking the pass buys Lecavalier time and space to execute his off-the-skate move, as any hesitation by a puck carrier can momentarily freeze a defender.

2 Wrists are rolled to bring the heel of the stick off the ice and the toe over the puck. Lecavalier can move his hands away from his body and further rotate his upper body to make it easier to direct the puck to his off skate.

3 Puck is behind the heel of the same-side skate and on the toe of the stick blade. When the off-side foot is down flat on the ice, Lecavalier will send the puck between his legs and bank it off his off skate.

The Vincent Lecavalier Special

A lot of players, like Pavel Datsyuk, Alex Kovalev and Ryan Getzlaf to name a few, have had success with this move, but perhaps none have used it as well as Vincent Lecavalier. Like the majority of skate dekes, this move is a pass to yourself that changes the position of the puck and the point of the attack. If executed properly, the Lecavalier Special will allow you to advance forward with the puck while eluding players and protecting the puck from stick checks.

Your goal with the Lecavalier Special is to move the puck through your legs from behind the heel of your same foot, off of your off foot, to a position in front of you on your backhand side. Start with the puck on your forehand side while you are skating toward a defender on your off side. Rotate your upper body far enough so that you are carrying the puck on your forehand behind the heel of your same skate: you should be traveling forward with your feet square to your direction of travel, your shoulders should almost face 90 degrees to your direction of travel on your forehand side and the puck should be to this side and behind you. Keep your head up.

Almost like the movement of a toe drag, bring the puck in toward the heel of your same skate with the front-side toe of your stick blade. From there, direct the puck between your legs off the inside edge of your off skate, and make sure that your skate blade is facing your direction of travel. You want the puck to deflect off your off skate and continue in front of your off foot. Once the puck is ahead of you, rotate your body to the front, collect the puck and continue driving on your off side.

By putting the puck through your legs and off the inside edge of your off skate, you can use your same foot to protect the puck from stick checks coming from your same side. Even if your pass misses your off skate, you are still moving the puck through your legs from behind the heel of your same foot to a position in front of you on your backhand side, which you can skate to—and you are still protecting the puck with your same foot.

The Lecavalier Special is very effective when used on a rush to your off side and combined with a fake shot, especially when the defender commits to blocking the shot, either by "stepping up" or going down in a shot-blocking position. It is also very effective during two-on-ones when you are on your off side. Here, as you move the puck behind to the heel of your same foot, you can fake a cross-ice pass to a teammate on your same side, execute the move and continue to drive around the defender on your backhand side.

Back Pass Variation

Carrying the puck on your forehand side behind your same skate and rotating your upper body allows you to fake a cross-ice pass to your same side. If you keep the puck on your forehand and rotate back a little further while angling your blade back, you can fake a pass to a trailing player. From this position it is easier to complete the Lecavalier Special with a pass off your skate from the back of your blade. Once you are rotated and your blade is angled as it would be for a pass to a trailer, lift your blade over the puck so the puck is on the back of your blade, then simply use the back of your blade to send the puck through your legs and off the inside of your off foot.

> ## Tip
>
> ✳ To practice the Lecavalier Special, skate in a circle (counterclockwise for lefties and clockwise for righties) with your skates on the circle but with your stick blade toward the middle of the circle, carrying the puck behind you. Repeatedly execute the move as you make your way around the circle.

Same Skate Variation

Another version of the Lecavalier Special is to pass the puck off the outside edge of your same skate instead of the inside edge of your off skate. When executing this variation you don't need to rotate your shoulders away from your line of travel as much as when doing the standard Lecavalier Special. The deflection off your same skate sends the puck ahead of you on your forehand side, instead of your on backhand side, as it would if the deflection were from your off skate.

Players most often use this variation as a fake before driving to their same side. The same skate variation adds an extra element of deception to the transition between the fake drive to your off side and the actual drive to your same side. With the puck staying on the forehand side, many players like to shoot or pass the puck quickly after this version of the Lecavalier Special, as it changes the angle of the shot or pass.

One-Handed Backhand Variation

Another variation of the Lecavalier Special starts with the puck on your off side. In this version, the puck is behind you and you are carrying it with one hand on your stick. Pass the puck between your legs and off your same skate (or off the outside edge of your off skate) with the back of your stick blade, and retrieve it in front of you and toward your off side. The difference when using the backhand is

that you cannot fake a shot or a pass since you only have one hand on your stick. You are also very vulnerable to checks as your body is open and turned away from your direction of travel. This backhand version is most effective when you accelerate quickly to your same side, decelerate and rotate your upper body while brining the puck behind you on your off side. Using the backhand skate move, you then direct the puck off your off skate or same skate to a point ahead of you on your off side. You can then accelerate to your off side to retrieve the puck and drive on your off side.

You can also use this variation when you over-skate the puck or when you need to retrieve a pass that is well behind you on your backhand side. If the puck is behind you, reach to your backhand side, direct the puck to your same skate or your off skate and deflect it in front of you to your off side. Bring your stick in front of you and retrieve the puck in one quick movement that allows you to keep your forward momentum. Keep your head up.

More Skate Moves

Fake Miss of the Puck

* You can also use skate moves and deceptive puck possession to create a gap in defensive coverage, such as by pretending to miss a loose puck in the corner or along the boards with your stick while skating forward, only to move it with the inside edge of your off skate up to your stick as you continue forward. In this instance you are using the "miss" of the puck with your stick to get the defender to hesitate and to momentarily relax the defensive coverage when it appears as though you have missed the puck. Accelerate immediately after you have moved the puck up to your stick to take advantage of the space you have gained through the defender's reaction.

The Pavel Bure

* To quickly change your shooting angle while carrying the puck in a normal puck-carrying position, pass the puck back between your skates to the inside edge of your off foot. Using the inside edge of your off skate, kick the puck past the heel of your same skate and back to your forehand side for a shot. Pavel Bure used this move very effectively to change shooting angles.

Backhand Skate Move After Over-Skating the Puck

Patrick Kane over-skates the puck and is about to retrieve it with a one-handed backhand pass to himself. Kane keeps his feet moving forward in the direction he is traveling in and rotates his upper body to allow his top hand to reach behind him with his stick. Commonly this pass is corralled and the puck is sent between the feet to a position where it can be picked up on the forehand side. Depending on the position of the defenders, the puck can also be directed off the same foot or off foot to a point ahead of him to his off side. Kane is left very vulnerable to an open-ice body check in this position, making this move very dangerous. Be sure to be aware of the situation around you before trying a play like this.

8 Breakaways

Kyle Okposo performs a right-handed Datsyuk deke. See page 140 for more on the Datsyuk deke.

Breakaway Basics

The first rule of any breakaway is that you must "read, react and take." That is, you must read the goalie's position (including the way the goalie adjusts to what you do), react to it and take advantage of what the goalie gives you.

It is important to keep an open mind when attacking a goalie on a breakaway and not decide beforehand what you are going to do, just as when you are deciding how to beat a defender during a rush. You may have a more set plan for a penalty shot or shootout, but even then you have to adapt and react to how the goalie plays you. Generally, if the goalie backs in, leaving more net, you should shoot; if the goalie is out, cutting down the angle and taking away your shot, he or she may be vulnerable to a deke. Speed will play an important factor in your decision making as well. If the goalie is well out from the net but backing up as you approach, you may want to adjust your speed by slowing down to see if the goalie continues to back in, leaving you more net to shoot at. If you are approaching the net with speed, the goalie might not react quickly enough and you may catch the goalie out too far, making it easier to deke. Don't forget that the goalie may do something unexpected in the course of the breakaway or penalty shot, such as

Speed is your Breakaway Ally
Rick Nash applies the breaks on Marty Turco, using a change of speed to get Turco out of position. Charging forward quickly and slowing down before a shoot or deke, as Nash does here, can move the goalie back into the net, creating more open space to shoot at. In this instance, Nash has Turco scrambling to stay close to the puck after having backed in too far.

sliding out or attempting a poke check. Be willing to improvise. Build up your toolbox of skills and draw from it, keep your options open and just let it happen.

Be in the Shooting Position

When you get into the "red zone," or scoring area, have the puck in a shooting position even if you might ultimately decide to deke. This way you still have the option to shoot. Mario Lemieux was a master at this. If you are in a scoring position

but have the puck in front of you and in the middle of your body, the goalie will sense a deke and react accordingly, as opposed to having to deal with the possibility of both a potential shot or a deke. There are many great dekes that start with the puck in a shooting position or involve a fake shot, giving you many options from this position. More importantly, even if you have decided to deke, the goalie may give you an opening at the last second, and if you are in a shooting position you will still

with the puck in shooting position can freeze the goalie, allowing you to move to your forehand or backhand side for a quick shot. A fake shot can be as subtle as rotating your top hand to open up your blade (sometimes referred to as a "show and go") or can involve imitating a shooting motion on your forehand or backhand side as illustrated on pages 111 and 116. Usually, once you have faked a shot and moved to your forehand or backhand, you should use an open-bladed shot to get the puck up and over the goalie, who will most likely be low to the ice, moving laterally to shut off the side of the net you are attacking. A fake shot with a quick move to your forehand or backhand (to change your shooting position) along with a quick release to an opening before the goalie can react is also a great move. You can do this move in close or out far, and you can shoot into an open side, up over the goalie or through an opening you created with your lateral attack, such as the five-hole.

have the option to shoot. Having said that, some players, like Sidney Crosby, are able to move the puck very quickly from a puckhandling position in front of them to a shooting position and release it quickly. However, the general rule is to start with the puck in a shooting position in order to keep your options open and the goalie guessing.

Fake Shots Score Big

A convincing fake shot is a great breakaway tool. Even a hesitation

The Same-Foot Fake Is Deadly

A fake shot from your same foot is particularly hard for a goalie to read because, with one foot raised off the ice, pressure on your stick and your shoulders square to the net, you are a threat to shoot at any time—and you can fake for as long as you can keep your balance since the puck is always in a shooting position. Once you decide to end the fake, you can drop your foot and shoot (off two feet) or move to your forehand or backhand side. Shooting remains an option throughout this fake, even until just before the point at which you move laterally off the fake.

Hesitation Creates Holes

You can freeze a goalie simply by mimicking a shooting position or quickly opening your blade and moving your top hand away from your body before you make a deke. This hesitation coupled with your hand and blade movement can create holes, as the goalie knows that you may actually shoot the puck using an open-bladed shot in close. Sometimes it will be easier to move the puck through a hole (like the five-hole) that the goalie has provided (by moving laterally) than it will be to maneuver all the way around the goalie.

Timing Your Release Is Key

Your distance from the net affects when you should release the puck. Goalies can move very well laterally, so gauge when to shoot. Should you shoot for a hole with a quick-release shot immediately after you move the puck laterally to change the shooting angle? Or do you have the room and time to wait until you are around the goalie so you can slip the puck into the open net? Remember, waiting may give the goalie a chance to move laterally and "close the door." It is also important to remember that the more fakes you use, the more time and space you need to execute them. Multiple fakes can be very effective, but you must start them early enough to give yourself the room to execute them. Pressure from checkers on a breakaway may dictate the number of fakes or fake options that are available to you.

Speed Is Your Breakaway Ally

Changes in speed of any kind create great opportunities to score goals. Charging forward quickly and slowing down before you shoot or deke can move the goalie back into the net, giving you more open space to shoot at. Moving in slowly and then accelerating as you approach the net may allow you to catch the goalie too far out of the net. Of course, on a breakaway your speed options will depend on how close the defenders are and what they are doing. However, on any breakaway, even a partial breakaway, you often have options as far as varying your speed in the red zone. Generally, it is much

more effective to move as quickly as you can while maintaining puck control. Moving at a higher speed gives you momentum through any deke, and it means that the deke can happen quicker, making it harder for the goalie to react and move across to cover the deke or a shot off a fake. It also means that you can slow down as part of your deception, something you can't do if you are already going slowly.

A great way to slow down when in close is to use a heel turn (see page 120). You can steer yourself in the direction you want by putting pressure on the heel of one of your skates. Heel turns are very effective when combined with lateral or vertical attack moves. Jason Spezza and Marian Gaborik are masters at the heel turn.

Players like Alex Kovalev have deceived goalies by changing the anticipated speed of a shot by winding up for a hard shot and then releasing it at half-speed, which is awkward for a goalie to adjust to. However, most openings will only be temporary, and a quick release with a fast shot is most effective.

Change Your Release Point

This is one of the simplest and most effective moves you can do. By quickly changing where the puck is before you shoot, either by pushing the puck out and away from your body, dragging it in, banking it off your skate or crossing it over your body laterally, you are altering (sometimes only slightly) your

shooting angle. If the goaltender does not respond to your puck movement, you will have open spaces to shoot at that weren't previously there. You can use puck movement when moving straight on the net or when on an angle. It is very effective when you are angling toward the net on your off side and moving the puck toward the center of the net, which will open up the net's far side. Similarly, it is effective when attacking from your proper side, when you can move the puck to the middle of the ice and release it on your backhand toward the far side of the net. The key is to change your shooting point quickly and release the puck quickly, before the goalkeeper has time to adjust.

Change Your Approach to the Net

Many players have had success on shootouts or penalty shots by approaching the net from an angle or on a curved approach, in particular by moving from their off side toward the middle of the ice. Sometimes players do this to set up a particular deke, like coming in on an angle from the off side to execute the Forsberg one-handed extension (see page 136) or the spinorama/tight turn move (see page 138) in close. At other times, players want to present a moving approach to see if the goalie makes a positioning mistake when adjusting to their approach, leaving an opening that the player can take advantage of.

Get the Puck Up Quickly

It is very important to be able to get the puck up quickly when you are in close. Goalies are becoming better and better at moving laterally and taking away the low part of the net. However, a quick lateral move off a fake with a quick shot into the top part of the net is very difficult for any goalie to stop. The open-bladed shot is great to get the puck up quickly off your forehand or backhand side. Some coaches call this shot a "3–11," meaning 3 feet, 11 inches—or just under the crossbar, which is 4 feet off the ice. Other coaches will ask their players to aim for the water bottle that invariably sits on top of the goalie's net. Either way the message is clear: when in close, get the puck up.

Double Dekes Can Beat Great Goalies

Double dekes are an excellent way to beat a goalie who has great anticipation and great lateral movement. The key to double faking is to start your move far enough away from the net that you still have room to get the puck up off your second deke if necessary. A very effective double fake involves a fake shot (forehand or backhand) followed by a lateral deke while moving to the opposite side before quickly returning to the side you originally faked from. Couple your fakes with the foot movements used when attacking laterally so you can accelerate when shifting direction, or, alternatively, use heel turns (see page 120) or outside edge reverses (see page 64) so you can slow down to give yourself more space to get the puck up.

The Forsberg

Perhaps the ultimate move used to change the position of the puck and the angle to the net is when players use one hand on their stick to extend their reach and change the position of the puck, the way Peter Forsberg famously did to defeat Canada and clinch gold for Sweden at the 1994 Lillehammer Olympics.

Method

You can attack the net straight on with this move, but it is much better to come in from an angle on your off wing, as the move relies heavily on lateral movement to create an opening for the puck. Start by attacking the net from your off side with the puck on your forehand side, and then drift into the middle of the ice so the puck is in the middle of the ice and your momentum is moving you from the near post to the far post. Once in

Second Generation
Anze Kopitar uses the Forsberg to score on Niklas Backstrom. Kopitar has executed the move earlier than Forsberg did in the photo to the left. It is likely that Kopitar's fake to shoot the puck to the far side of the net (Backstrom's stick side) was so successful that Kopitar didn't have to move as far to his same side as Forsberg did before finishing the move.

Notes

Even if a goalie has bought your fake and is down on the far side, it doesn't mean he or she is out. Be mindful of a poke check as you bring the puck from your forehand to your backhand. As well, if you don't shift the goalie far enough over to the far side, he or she may still be able to make a desperate lunge back to the near side to block the puck; in this scenario you may need to get the puck up off the ice to beat the goalie. Skilled players are able to raise the puck even when shooting off a one-handed extended reach on their backhand. Be sure to roll your wrist to elevate the puck when you shoot it.

the middle, fake a shot to the far side of the net, freezing the goalie momentarily. Remember to sell the fake with your body, stick and, most importantly, your eyes.

As you fake, move across the net to the far side as if to deke to your forehand side, but start to move the puck to your backhand, against the flow of your movement, and ultimately extend your reach all the way to your backhand with only one hand on your stick. Your body, and most likely the goalie, will end up near the far post, while your reach will enable you to extend your arm across the crease for a tap into the open part of the net.

Against very skilled goalies, who might anticipate this move, you can fake a shot to the far post and then extend your reach with the puck to your forehand side before

moving the puck against the flow to your backhand side. This extra puckhandling will force the goalie to track the puck to the far post, leaving the near side of the net wide open. If your fake shot is good enough to freeze the goalie, it may cause the goalkeeper to make a desperate attempt to stay with you as you advance on the forehand to the far post, leaving you with even more net on the near side.

The Spinorama

Spinorama Backhand Release

Jason Blake beats Scott Clemmensen with a spinorama. Blake started his move with speed and on an angle from his off side (Clemmensen's glove side; the near side of the net). As he approached the far side of the goal, Blake executed a lateral slide with his back facing the goalie. From his lateral slide, Blake then executed a tight turn to the backhand to spin his body around so he could fire the puck on his backhand into the near side of the net.

This move is also known as the Savardian Spinorama, named after NHL greats Serge Savard and Denis Savard. Both players used the move as a deke around opposing players to get to open ice or to the goal, but it was seldom used directly on goalies. Today, players like Pierre-Marc Bouchard and Jason Blake have popularized the move as a shootout option.

Method

A Spinorama is best when executed with speed coming from an angle on your off side. Attack the net with the puck on your forehand side and skate hard toward the far side post, selling the shot to the far side the entire way. As you get right in on the goal, you should be closer to the far side than to the near side, put the puck on your backhand side and initiate a lateral slide with your rear toward the net.

From your lateral slide you need to execute a tight turn to your backhand side, bringing the puck away from the goalie and back to the near side of the net. The goalie should be down and out, having moved with you laterally toward the far side of the net, leaving the near side open for you to slip the puck into the net on your backhand as you come out of your tight turn.

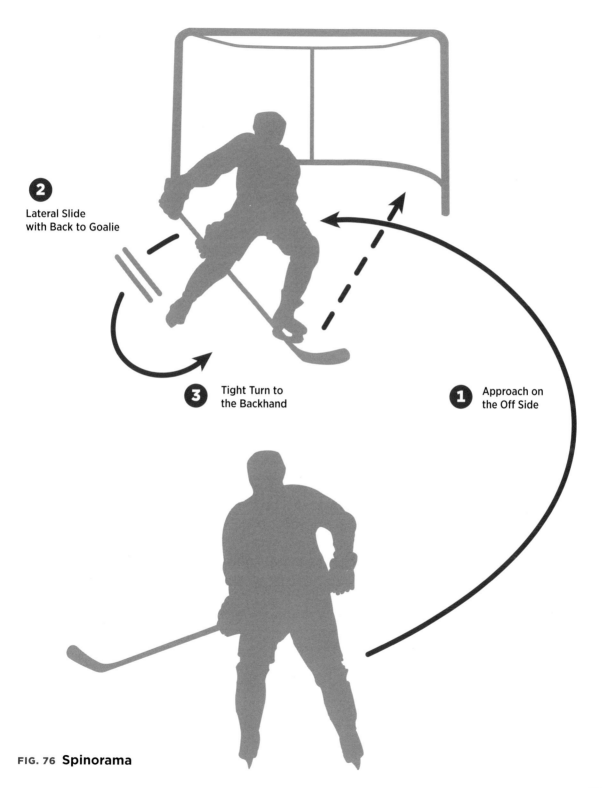

2 Lateral Slide with Back to Goalie

3 Tight Turn to the Backhand

1 Approach on the Off Side

FIG. 76 Spinorama

The Datsyuk

As dekes become more popular and the shootout continues to be an important part of NHL action, players have begun to introduce new and innovative moves to their list of possible ways to beat goalies. Pavel Datsyuk's signature vertical and lateral move is a great example of a how a skilled player can combine existing elements to create something new and effective.

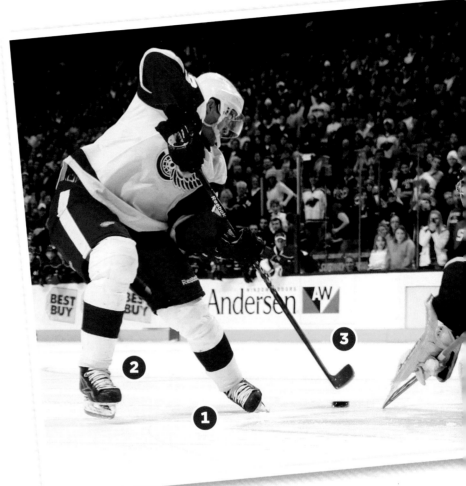

It's best to start this move as a straightaway attack with speed. As you reach the hash marks in the slot, pull the puck back on your forehand side and fake a same-foot shot to the near side of the net (stick side for left-handed players, trapper side for right-handed players). Raise your off foot from the ice during the same-foot fake shot to help sell the fake, and push the puck forward as though you are going to release it toward the near side of the net. When you reach the release point of the shot, don't pull the trigger; instead, push your top hand away from your body, lift

The Datsyuk
Angling Away from the Goalie

Pavel Datsyuk executes his signature move against Josh Harding. Datsyuk started his move with a straightaway attack and a fake same-foot shot to the near side (Harding's glove side).

1 Datsyuk is currently in the middle of his move, where he is angling his same foot toward his off side, sending him away from Harding and toward the far side of the net.

2 His off foot is returning to the ice from its elevated position during the same-foot fake. This will help him to glide.

3 He lifts the blade of his stick over the puck so he can handle it on his backhand. Datsyuk will then continue to glide toward his off side (the far side of the net), dragging the puck with him on his backhand, until he is clear of Harding, at which point Datsyuk will put the puck on his forehand and raise it into the net.

Practicing the Datsyuk Drag

Assume the hockey-playing position. Place a glove on the ice two to three feet in front of your same skate and place a puck on the ice between your skate and your glove. With your skates stationary, handle the puck around the glove. First, move the puck with the front of your blade around the outside of the glove. When you get to the top of the glove, push your top hand away from your body and lift your blade over the puck. Now drag the puck on the backside of your blade around the top and the inside of the glove, until you reach your original position. Repeat.

FIG. 77

Angling Away: Front View

This is the front view of the Datsyuk as you angle your same foot toward your off side and away from the goalie (the far side of the net). When you drag the puck on your backhand across the crease, remember to bring it away from the goalie and toward your same-side heel.

your stick over the puck and drag the puck toward you with the back of your blade. At the same time, pivot your same skate so the toe angles toward your off side, and glide on this angled skate across the front of the net, toward the far side and away from your fake. This should move you away from the goalie and toward the open net on the far side, as the goalie will be recovering from your fake to the near side.

To avoid a poke check and to get around the goalie while moving to the far side, drag the puck slightly behind your same heel—your

body from the torso up will be rotated much the same way that it is during the Lecavalier Special (see page 127). As you begin to move further to the far side, you can bring your off foot down, creating a weight transfer, which will help you glide to the far side. When clear of the goalie (at which point you will be almost beside the far-side post), lift your stick over the puck to place the puck on the front of your blade and shoot it into the net on your forehand. By the time you have the puck on your forehand and have worked your way across the

goalmouth, the goaltender should be down and out on the other side of the net, leaving you with a wide-open cage. However, beware of a last-ditch dive across the net from the goalie—get that puck up.

Glossary

BACKHAND SIDE Opposite to your same side. Your stick blade will be away from this side of your body when you are set up in the hockey-playing position.

BACK SKATE The skate farthest from your target when you are shooting (or passing) in a traditional manner; the skate farthest from the object you are moving toward when doing a lateral slide.

BALL OF THE FOOT The somewhat circular mound at the bottom of your foot, at the base of your big toe.

BLADE OF THE STICK SQUARE TO THE ICE Holding or moving your stick in a position such that the greatest portion of the bottom of the blade is on the ice.

BLADE RADIUS The contour or profile of the blade.

BODY SQUARE TO THE OBJECT (OR A DIRECTION) Positioning your body such that your shoulders and upper torso are facing the object or direction.

BOTTOM HAND Your same-side hand, which holds the shaft of your stick below your top hand (or the top of the stick).

BREAK(ING) YOUR WRISTS The motion of rotating both your top and bottom hands while shooting or passing the puck so that the stick's blade moves from a closed position while holding the puck to an open position and then quickly to a closed position when releasing the puck; also very extreme rotation of your wrists.

CENTERLINE OF THE BODY An imaginary line dividing the body in half lengthwise, from top to bottom.

CLOSED BLADE For a right-handed player: the blade of your stick, starting from a position square on the ice, is rotated to create an angle to the ice of less than 90 degrees when the backhand side of your blade faces the ice and greater than 90 degrees when the forehand side of your blade faces the ice. For a left-handed player: the blade of your stick, starting from a position square on the ice, is rotated to create an angle to the ice of less than 90 degrees when the forehand side of your blade faces the ice and greater than 90 degrees when the backhand side of your blade faces the ice.

CYCLE OF POWER The full movement of the drive skate through one cycle during a particular skating technique.

DRIVE The combined force of a leg and skate pushing down toward the ice and away from the body.

FAR SIDE Relative to a player, the side of the net farthest from the player.

FEET SQUARE TO THE OBJECT (OR A DIRECTION) Positioning your feet such that your toes are facing the object or direction.

FLAT BLADE A "perfectly" flat skate blade—you are on a skate blade that is flat from front to back and from side to side.

FLAT BLADE, FRONT TO BACK Your weight is evenly distributed over the entire length of your skate blade, from the ball of your foot (front) to your heel (back).

FLAT BLADE, SIDE TO SIDE Your weight (and the pressure you apply) is evenly distributed over the inside and outside edges of your skate blade.

FOREHAND SIDE The proper side (or same side); the side opposite your offside. This is the side you shoot from when taking a forehand shot, and it is the side your stick blade will be on when you are set up in the hockey-playing position.

FRONT SKATE The skate closest to your target when you are shooting (or passing) in a traditional manner; the skate closest to the object you are moving toward when doing a lateral slide.

HEEL OF THE BLADE The bottom of the blade; the part of the blade that is closest to the connection of the blade to the shaft.

HEEL OF THE FOOT The pad at the bottom of your foot, at the back of your foot.

HOCKEY-PLAYING POSITION The basic stance for playing hockey when you have two hands on your stick.

HOCKEY-SKATING POSITION The basic stance for skating when you have one hand on your stick.

HOLLOW The concave groove between the two edges of your skate blade.

INSIDE EDGE OF THE SKATE BLADE The edge of the skate blade that is closest to the inside of your skate and foot (the same side as your big toe).

LATERAL ATTACK MOVE Any deke where you combine a lateral movement with forward motion to go around, or separate from, a player.

LATERAL (HORIZONTAL) WEIGHT TRANSFER Having your weight over one skate and then shifting or moving your weight so that it is over the other skate.

MOVING TO THE OFF SIDE Moving to the side away from the way you shoot (i.e., a right-handed player moving to the left; a left-handed player moving to the right).

NEAR SIDE Relative to a player, the side of the net closest to the player.

OFF FOOT OR SKATE The foot that is opposite to your proper (same) side (i.e., the left foot for a right-handed player; the right foot for a left-handed player).

OFF SIDE The side opposite your (proper) same side, (i.e., the left side for a right-handed player; the right side for a left-handed player).

OPENING THE BLADE For a right-handed player: the blade of your stick, starting from a position square on the ice, is rotated to create an angle to the ice of less than 90 degrees when the forehand side of your blade faces the ice and greater than 90 degrees when the backhand side of your blade faces the ice. For a left-handed player: the blade of your stick, starting from a position square on the ice, is rotated to create an angle to the ice of less than 90 degrees when the backhand side of your blade faces the ice and greater than 90 degrees when the forehand side of your blade faces the ice.

OUTSIDE EDGE OF THE BLADE The edge of the skate blade closest to the outside of your skate and foot (the same side as your pinky toe).

PAD OF THE FOOT The mound or pad on the bottom of your foot that runs along the base of all your toes—from the circular mound at the base of the big toe (the ball of the foot) to the mound under the pinky toe (the metatarsal pad).

PITCH OF THE SKATE The angle of the bottom of the foot in the skate relative to the blade of the skate.

PROPER SIDE Opposite to the off side (i.e., the right side for a right-handed player; the left side for a left-handed player).

RADIUS OF HOLLOW (ROH) The depth of the hollow between the two edges of your skate blade.

RECOVERY After the drive and thrust, bringing the drive skate back to its original position to repeat the cycle of power.

ROTATION OF THE TOP HAND Turning the wrist of the top hand while holding the stick with the proper grip, causing the blade to open or close.

SAME SIDE Opposite to the off side (i.e., the right side for a right-handed player; the left side for a left-handed player).

SAME FOOT OR SKATE The foot that is opposite to your off side, (i.e., the right foot for a right-handed player; the left foot for a left-handed player).

TOE OF THE STICK BLADE The end of the stick blade, farthest from where the blade connects to the shaft.

TOP HAND The hand at the top of the shaft of the stick.

TRADITIONAL SHOT/PASS Shooting or passing with your feet facing 90 degrees to your target. Your weight is carried from your back foot (same foot) to your front foot (off foot) when on your forehand, and from the back foot (off foot) to your front foot (same foot) when on your backhand.

Acknowledgments

I sincerely want to thank the following people, without whom this book would not have been the same:

STEVE CAMERON—my editor, for your countless hours and incredible patience; for your dedication in finding that perfect photograph; for all the time at the rink; and for understanding and embracing the message. You have brought this all to life! I can't thank you enough.

HOWIE MEEKER—for your boundless energy and passion for teaching. It was a privilege to have you as a mentor and to work with you and your sons for over a decade. Your enthusiasm for the game was contagious. Thank you for the start you gave me.

BOBBY SMITH—as an NHL player you had that rare combination of elite skills and knowledge with the ability to teach. You have never lost sight of the importance of having fun on the ice. Thanks for everything you brought to UltraSkills!

RON MacLEAN—working with you was an absolute pleasure. You are a true ambassador for our game and have used a national platform unselfishly for the betterment of hockey. Thank you for helping so many people to connect to hockey in such a positive way and, in particular, for your support for what I do. You are a real inspiration!

CYRIL LEEDER—thanks for that unforgettable call in the middle of the night to tell me that you had come up with the perfect costume for "UltraMan … Bullseye!" You have lived the passion with me Cy—and we have always been on the same page. Thanks for always being there for me and for everything you have done for hockey in Ottawa.

BRIAN KILREA—it was a pleasure to play for you coach! You taught me the most important hockey lesson: have fun every time you are on the ice. It is a lesson I have never forgotten. I had fun every practice and game with you behind the bench. Thanks for making a difference, Killer!

CRAIG JENKINS—I have not met anyone who can teach puckhandling and scoring skills better than you. You are a gifted teacher. I learn from you every time we are on the ice together. Thank you for being a part of UltraSkills and for allowing me to be a part of Excel Hockey.

NIGEL LESTER—you were my lead instructor when I started at Howie's in 1974. We have taught together for over three decades. Thanks for everything you gave, every year, to UltraSkills.

DAVE KONAROWSKI—your love for skates and blades and your knowledge of the impact they have is unrivalled. Your passion hits me whenever I walk into Crow's. Don't ever lose it!

MOM AND DAD—for introducing me to this incredible game, for driving me to the rink a million times, for taking me to see Canada play the Soviets when I was 10 and planting the seed of my dream to play for my country—and then encouraging me to pursue that dream … For everything that you did for so many years… I will always be grateful.

Ron Davidson and his family. Top row (from left): Ron and Lauren; middle row (from left): Taryn, Lynn, Sean and Talia.

JAMES AND JOHN —for the hours we spent playing shinny, hoping time would stand still. For experiencing, with me, the game the way it was meant to be played, and for our never ending discussions about hockey. At the corner rink we lived the dream together—may we always…

MY FAMILY—I simply can't do justice to how grateful I am for everything you have done to allow me to pursue my passion. Thank you, Lynn, for your incredible support and encouragement. It has meant so much to me. You made UltraSkills possible, and *Play Better Hockey* would never have happened without your support. And to Talia, Lauren, Taryn and Sean. I can't thank you enough for sharing this passion with me. I have loved coaching you and watching you play. Remember, I am your biggest fan! May you continue to enjoy this wonderful game for many years to come!